Words of Praise for
BELOVED

It is my hope that this book ... ... ry of prayer, will be a valuable ... ... a deeper and more vibrant relationship with the triune God.

> —Most Reverend Paul S. Loverde, Bishop of Arlington

This beautiful and extensive prayer book should be placed in every Catholic home and parish library. I highly recommend it!

> —Donna-Marie Cooper O'Boyle,
> EWTN television host and author of numerous
> books, including *The Miraculous Medal: Stories,
> Prayers, and Devotions*

A powerful compilation of prayers for all states of soul and mind and all major life situations.

> —Michael H. Brown, founder of SpiritDaily.com and
> author of numerous books, including *Fear of Fire*

Prayer is essential. *Beloved* is a wonderful collection of powerful prayers handed down to us through the centuries.

> —Tom Peterson, founder and president of Catholics
> Come Home Inc. and VirtueMedia, and author of
> *Catholics Come Home*

Prayer is the life of the soul. It gives strength to the weary, comfort to the sorrowful, and makes a person fall deeply in love with God. It is for this reason that *Beloved: A Collection of Timeless Catholic Prayers* is a perfect book—and a much needed one—for the twenty-first century. This book will give us strength, comfort, and help us all fall in love with God again!

—Fr. Donald Calloway, MIC,
author of *Under the Mantle: Marian Thoughts From a 21st Century Priest* and *No Turning Back: A Witness to Mercy*

I strongly endorse *Beloved: A Collection of Timeless Catholic Prayers*. This book will aid the saint, the sinner, the beginner, and those who have been Catholic their entire life get closer to God.

—Fr. Stefan Starzynski,
author of *Miracles: Healing for a Broken World*

BELOVED

A Collection of
Timeless Catholic Prayers

MARGARET M. DVORAK

Liguori
LIGUORI, MISSOURI

Imprimi Potest: Harry Grile, CSsR, Provincial, Denver Province, The Redemptorists

Published by Liguori Publications, Liguori, Missouri 63057

To order, call 800-325-9521
www.liguori.org

Library of Congress Cataloging-in-Publication Data

Dvorak, Margaret M.

    Beloved : a collection of timeless Catholic prayers / Margaret M. Dvorak.
    —First Edition .
    pages cm

1. Catholic Church—Prayers and devotions. I. Title.
    BX2149.2.D86 2014
    242'.802—dc23

                                     2013044750

p ISBN: 978-0-7648-2394-7
e ISBN: 978-0-7648-6879-5

For more information on sources, see the author's note on page 8.

Liguori Publications, a nonprofit corporation, is an apostolate of The Redemptorists. To learn more about The Redemptorists, visit Redemptorists.com.

Printed in the United States of America
18 17 16 15 14 / 5 4 3 2 1
First Edition

This book is dedicated with love
to my husband, Bill, and
my son, Will.

I can do all things in him who strengthens me.
PHILIPPIANS 4:13

Through the Immaculate Heart of Mary

ACKNOWLEDGMENTS

A heartfelt thank you to Liguori Publications. My deepest appreciation to acquisitions editor Theresa Nienaber, publicist Mary Brockgreitens, and most especially former acquisitions editor Erin Cartaya.

My thanks also to Reverend Mother Anne of Jesus, OCD, and all the dear sisters at the Carmelite Monastery in Des Plaines, Illinois, and to Sr. Mary Terzo, FMA, and Sr. Rosalie Di Piero, FMA, of the Salesian Sisters of St. John Bosco in Haledon, New Jersey, and to my family and friends. I am grateful for all your love, encouragement, support, and prayers.

To the Blessed Mother, Queen of the Holy Rosary: Thank you for that moment of grace so many years ago when I was inspired to pray the rosary. I knew in that moment I would pray the rosary every day for the rest of my life.

CONTENTS

From the Author: This prayer book was compiled from sources that include internet websites, old prayer books, prayer leaflets, booklets, church bulletins, Mass cards, and holy cards, all of which I have been collecting most of my life. I have made every effort to contact copyright holders for permissions.

INTRODUCTION

Praised Be Jesus Christ!

The prayers and devotions I share with you come from the rich tradition of the Catholic Church. It is a beautiful collection of vocal prayers that will bring you comfort, hope, and strength while deepening your faith and love for God. These prayers are a gift from God to us—his beloved children. They are to be loved and cherished, shared with others, and passed down from generation to generation.

Included here are prayers that will lift your heart and mind to God—prayers that offer praise, adoration, and thanksgiving to our heavenly Father. You will find traditional prayers to the Holy Trinity, Jesus and the Holy Spirit, along with prayers to St. Joseph and the Blessed Mother asking them to intercede for us. There are also prayers for a variety of occasions that may be prayed in order or chosen individually for your own specific spiritual or temporal needs. Then there are prayers written by the saints and inspired by the Holy Spirit that can lead us to the same graces sought by these holy men and women when we struggle to carry life's crosses. They are profound and heartfelt prayers that will help us grow closer to Jesus.

The rosary, the Stations of the Cross, the chaplets, and other devotional prayers are presented to you with Scripture I've found personally inspiring. Praying with Scripture benefits both those desiring to understand Scripture more deeply and those who are looking for a way to keep their prayer life from becoming mundane by presenting these classic prayers in the context of the mysteries of our faith. In the book *The Way of Perfection*, St. Teresa of Ávila suggests that vocal prayers, like those found in this book, can lead us to deep, contemplative prayer: "All prayer begins with vocal prayer—such as the Our Father and the Hail Mary—then by meditation on the meaning of what is being said, the soul will be led to contemplative prayer."

These prayers and my accompanying Scripture selection will help lead you to the kind of contemplative prayer St. Teresa speaks about.

We may pray the same prayers over the span of our lives, but their meanings can change with our life experiences. There may be a day when you are facing a particularly difficult situation and the Chaplet of St. Michael takes on a special meaning. After praying the chaplet you may be inspired to pray in your own words, asking the holy angels to protect you and guide you. Another day, a Scripture verse or short aspiration may speak to your heart. I would suggest you make a copy of the prayer, tape it up on your kitchen window or anywhere you will see it often, and let it brighten up your day!

Whether you have been praying for years or are just starting out your prayer life, I pray that this collection of timeless Catholic prayers and devotions will inspire you, touch you, bring you joy, and lead you to love God with all your heart.

May God abundantly bless you and your loved ones today and always.

MARGARET M. DVORAK
"MARY, MOTHER OF GOD, PRAY FOR US."

THE HOLY ROSARY

Of all the prayers, the rosary is the most beautiful and the richest in grace; of all, it is the most pleasing to Mary, the Virgin Most Holy. Therefore, love the rosary and recite it every day with devotion.

ATTRIBUTED TO POPE ST. PIUS X

"Rosary" comes from the Latin word *rosarium*, meaning "garland of roses" or "crown of roses." We offer a spiritual "bouquet of roses" to the Blessed Mother every time we pray the rosary. Mary lovingly intercedes for each one of us as she presents our intentions before the throne of God to her Son, Jesus. Our prayers are always answered. Perhaps not as we expected (or desired) them to be, but "no prayer ever went unheard and our Blessed Lady has never been known to fail," to quote *Rosary Novenas to Our Lady*.

The rosary is a simple and beautiful prayer that brings reconciliation, peace and inner joy. It was a favorite prayer of Blessed Pope John Paul II*. "From my youthful years this prayer has held an important place in my spiritual life....The rosary has accompanied me in moments of joy and in moments of difficulty. To it I

* Blessed Pope John Paul II and Blessed Pope John XXIII were scheduled to be canonized on April 27, 2014.

have entrusted any number of concerns; in it I have always found comfort," Blessed John Paul II wrote in his apostolic letter *Rosarium Virginis Mariae*. He also wrote, "To recite the Rosary is nothing other than to contemplate with Mary the face of Christ....The Rosary helps us to be conformed ever more closely to Christ until we attain true holiness." When you pray the rosary, with all your heart, the Pope said, you will experience an "outpouring of the Holy Spirit."

After the Holy Sacrifice of the Mass and the Liturgy of the Hours, the rosary is the highest form of prayer to praise God. It is considered to be a perfect prayer because it is both a mental and a vocal prayer. The rosary is divided into four different sets of Mysteries (Joyful, Luminous, Sorrowful, and Glorious), and each set has five decades. Each decade represents an event in the life of Jesus. The scriptural rosary is a powerful way to pray the rosary, because it provides Scripture verses from the Bible for each Hail Mary. As much as possible, the verses are then blended together to tell the story of each mystery. Thus, it brings each mystery to life. While praying the rosary, you contemplate the joys, sorrows, and glories of Jesus with Mary. Within the rosary is the story of our salvation, too.

The rosary is one of the most cherished prayers of the Catholic Church. It is loved and recommended by saints, popes, priests, and countless others. The month of October is dedicated to the Holy Rosary, which includes the feast of Our Lady of the Rosary on October 7.

HOW TO PRAY THE ROSARY

Many people pray all four sets of mysteries (Joyful, Luminous, Sorrowful, and Glorious) of the rosary every day. Traditionally, most people pray one set of mysteries (five decades) each day, praying the Joyful Mysteries on Mondays and Saturdays, the Sorrowful Mysteries on Tuesdays and Fridays, the Luminous Mysteries on Thursdays, and the Glorious Mysteries on Wednesdays and Sundays.

~ *St. Louis de Montfort encourages us:*

"Recite your rosary with faith, with humility, with confidence, and with perseverance."

After the Sign of the Cross and/or after each mystery is announced, you can "offer" your rosary to our Blessed Mother for her intentions (for example, I offer this rosary my dear Mother for your intentions) or for a particular intention of your own (for example, I offer this decade for my family).

~ *St. Louise de Marillac suggests:*

"Commend your children to the Immaculate Heart of Mary. When parents pray the rosary, at the end of each decade they should hold the rosary aloft and say to her, 'With these beads bind my children to Your Immaculate Heart.' She will attend to their souls."

Some examples of intentions are:

For the pope, bishops, and priests and all in religious life....

For all those who need prayers and have no one to pray for them....

For all those I have hurt during my life....

For the sick, suffering, and for those who will die today....

For the souls in purgatory (names of loved ones) and especially the forgotten souls....

For my sister, Anne, who was diagnosed with breast cancer....
For my daughter, Sarah, as she studies for her final exams....
For my neighbor John, who is unemployed....

~ *Sr. Lucia de Santos (1917 Fatima visionary) reminds us:*
"There is no problem, I tell you, no matter how difficult it is, that we cannot solve by the prayer of the Holy Rosary."

There are times when we have so much on our mind—our thoughts can easily wander away to our worries or concerns. There are also times when we have nothing particular on our mind, and yet our thoughts still wander away. When praying the scriptural rosary, the Scripture verses help keep your mind from distractions. It keeps your focus on Jesus.

~ *St. Thérèse of Lisieux helps us:*
"I, too, have distractions, but as soon as I perceive the distractions, I pray for the persons who come into my imagination, and so they draw benefit from my distraction."

HOW TO PRAY THE ROSARY

1. On the crucifix, make the Sign of the Cross and pray the Apostles' Creed.
2. On the first single bead next to the crucifix, pray the Our Father.
3. On the next three beads, pray a Hail Mary (for an increase in the virtues of faith, hope, and charity)
4. On the last single bead, pray the Glory Be.
4b. Announce the first mystery and pray the Our Father on that same single bead.
5. Pray one Hail Mary on each of the ten beads.
6. On the space between the last bead of the decade and the single bead between the decades, pray the Glory Be and Oh my Jesus.
7. On the single bead between the decades, announcing the next mystery, pray the Our Father.
8. Follow steps 5 and 6 for the remaining mysteries.
9. Pray the Hail, Holy Queen, then any optional prayers after the rosary.
10. Make the Sign of the Cross to conclude.

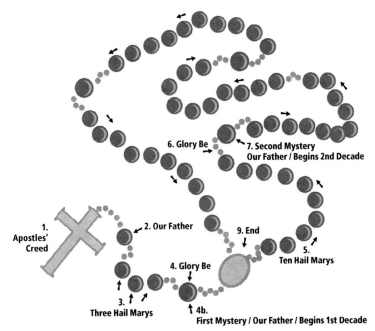

6. Glory Be

7. Second Mystery
Our Father / Begins 2nd Decade

1.
Apostles'
Creed

2. Our Father

9. End

5.
Ten Hail Marys

4. Glory Be

3.
Three Hail Marys

4b.
First Mystery / Our Father / Begins 1st Decade

THE PRAYERS OF THE ROSARY

The Apostles' Creed

I believe in God,
the Father almighty,
Creator of heaven and earth,
and in Jesus Christ, his only Son, our Lord,
who was conceived by the Holy Spirit,
born of the Virgin Mary,
suffered under Pontius Pilate,
was crucified, died and was buried;
he descended into hell;
on the third day he rose again from the dead;
he ascended into heaven,
and is seated at the right hand of God the Father almighty;
from there he will come to judge the living and the dead.

I believe in the Holy Spirit,
the holy catholic Church,
the communion of saints,
the forgiveness of sins,
the resurrection of the body,
and life everlasting.
Amen.

The Our Father

Our Father, who art in heaven,
hallowed be thy name;
thy kingdom come;
thy will be done on earth as it is in heaven.

Give us this day our daily bread;
and forgive us our trespasses
as we forgive those who trespass
against us;
and lead us not into temptation,
but deliver us from evil.
Amen.

The Hail Mary

Hail Mary, full of grace, the Lord is with you;
blessed are you among women,
and blessed is the fruit of your womb, Jesus.
Holy Mary, Mother of God,
pray for us sinners
now and at the hour of our death.
Amen.

The Glory Be (The Doxology)

Glory be to the Father, the Son, and the Holy Spirit;
as it was in the beginning, is now, and ever shall be,
world without end.
Amen.

The Fatima Prayer

O my Jesus, forgive us our sins, save us from the fires of hell, lead
all souls to heaven, especially those most in need of Thy Mercy.

> ~ *This prayer was requested by Our Blessed Mother*
> *at Fatima in 1917.*

THE JOYFUL MYSTERIES

The First Joyful Mystery:
The Annunciation

The fruit of the mystery is humility.

~ I offer this decade for (say your intention).

Our Father

"In the sixth month, the angel Gabriel was sent from God to a town of Galilee called Nazareth, to a virgin betrothed to a man named Joseph, of the house of David, and the virgin's name was Mary" (Luke 1:26–27).

Hail Mary

"And coming to her, he said, 'Hail, favored one! The Lord is with you'" (Luke 1:28).

Hail Mary

"But she was greatly troubled at what was said and pondered what sort of greeting this might be. Then the angel said to her, 'Do not be afraid, Mary, for you have found favor with God'" (Luke 1:29–30).

Hail Mary

"Behold, you will conceive in your womb and bear a son, and you shall name him Jesus. He will be great and will be called Son of the Most High...." (Luke 1:31–32).

Hail Mary

"...And the Lord God will give him the throne of David his father, and he will rule over the house of Jacob forever, and of his kingdom there will be no end" (Luke 1:32–33).

Hail Mary

"But Mary said to the angel, 'How can this be, since I have no relations with a man?'" (Luke 1:34).

Hail Mary

"And the angel said to her in reply, 'The Holy Spirit will come upon you, and the power of the Most High will overshadow you'" (Luke 1:35).

Hail Mary

"Therefore the child to be born will be called holy, the Son of God" (Luke 1:35).

Hail Mary

"And behold, Elizabeth, your relative, has also conceived a son in her old age; and this is the sixth month with her who was called barren. For nothing will be impossible for God" (Luke 1:36–37).

Hail Mary

"Mary said, 'Behold, I am the handmaid of the Lord. May it be done to me according to your word.' Then the angel departed from her" (Luke 1:38).

Hail Mary, Glory Be, Oh my Jesus

The Second Joyful Mystery:
The Visitation

The fruit of the mystery is love of neighbor.

~ I offer this decade for (say your intention).

Our Father

"During those days Mary set out and traveled to the hill country in haste to a town of Judah, where she entered the house of Zechariah and greeted Elizabeth" (Luke 1:39–40).

Hail Mary

"When Elizabeth heard Mary's greeting, the infant leaped in her womb, and Elizabeth, filled with the holy Spirit, cried out in a loud voice and said, 'Most blessed are you among women, and blessed is the fruit of your womb'" (Luke 1:41–42).

Hail Mary

"And how does this happen to me, that the mother of my Lord should come to me? For at the moment the sound of your greeting reached my ears, the infant in my womb leaped for joy" (Luke 1:43–44).

Hail Mary

"Blessed are you who believed that what was spoken to you by the Lord would be fulfilled" (Luke 1:45).

Hail Mary

"And Mary said: 'My soul proclaims the greatness of the Lord; my spirit rejoices in God my savior. For he has looked upon his handmaid's lowliness'" (Luke 1:46–48).

Hail Mary

"Behold, from now on all will all ages call me blessed. The Mighty One has done great things for me, and holy is his name" (Luke 1:48–49).

Hail Mary

"His mercy is from age to age to those who fear him. He has shown might with his arm, dispersed the arrogant of mind and heart" (Luke 1:50–51).

Hail Mary

"He has thrown down the rulers from their thrones but lifted up the lowly. The hungry he has filled with good things; the rich he has sent away empty" (Luke 1:52–53).

Hail Mary

"He has helped Israel his servant, remembering his mercy, according to his promise to our fathers, to Abraham and to his descendants forever" (Luke 1:54–55).

Hail Mary

"Mary remained with her about three months and then returned to her home" (Luke 1:56).

Hail Mary, Glory Be, Oh my Jesus

The Third Joyful Mystery:
The Nativity

The fruit of the mystery is detachment of things.

~ I offer this decade for (say your intention).

Our Father

"Now this is how the birth of Jesus Christ came about. When his mother Mary was betrothed to Joseph, but before they lived together, she was found with child through the holy Spirit" (Matthew 1:18).

Hail Mary

"Joseph her husband, since he was a righteous man, yet unwilling to expose her to shame, decided to divorce her quietly" (Matthew 1:19).

Hail Mary

"Such was his intention when, behold, the angel of the Lord, appeared to him in a dream and said, 'Joseph, son of David, do not be afraid to take Mary your wife into your home. For it is through the holy Spirit that this child has been conceived in her. She will bear a son and you are to name him Jesus, because he will save his people from their sins'" (Matthew 1:20–21).

Hail Mary

"All this took place to fulfill what the Lord had said through the prophet: 'Behold, the virgin shall be with child and bear a son, and they shall name him Emmanuel,' which means 'God is with us.' When Joseph awoke, he did as the angel of the Lord had commanded him and took his wife into his home" (Matthew 1:22–24).

Hail Mary

"In those days a decree went out from Caesar Augustus that the whole world should be enrolled....And Joseph...went up from Galilee from the town of Nazareth to Judea, to the city of David that is called Bethlehem, because he was of the house and family of David, to be enrolled with Mary, his betrothed, who was with child" (Luke 2:1, 4–5).

Hail Mary

"While they were there, the time came for her to have her child, and she gave birth to her firstborn son. She wrapped him in swaddling clothes and laid him in a manger, because there was no room for them in the inn" (Luke 2:6–7).

Hail Mary

"Now there were shepherds in that region living in the fields and keeping the night watch over their flock. The angel of the Lord appeared to them and the glory of the Lord shone around them, and they were struck with great fear" (Luke 2:8–9).

Hail Mary

"The angel said to them, 'Do not be afraid; for behold, I proclaim to you good news of great joy that will be for all the people. For today in the city of David a savior has been born for you who is Messiah and Lord. And this will be a sign for you: you will find an infant wrapped in swaddling clothes and lying in a manger'" (Luke 2:10–12).

Hail Mary

"And suddenly there was a multitude of the heavenly host with the angel, praising God and saying: 'Glory to God in the highest and on earth peace to those on whom his favor rests'" (Luke 2:13–14).

Hail Mary

"So they went in haste and found Mary and Joseph, and the infant lying in the manger. When they saw this, they made known the message that had been told them about this child.... And Mary kept all these things, reflecting on them in her heart" (Luke 2:16–17, 19).

Hail Mary, Glory Be, Oh my Jesus

The Fourth Joyful Mystery:
The Presentation

The fruit of the mystery is obedience.
~ I offer this decade for (say your intention).

Our Father

"When the days were completed for [Mary and Joseph's] purification according to the law of Moses, they took him up to Jerusalem to present him to the Lord..." (Luke 2:22).

Hail Mary

"...To offer the sacrifice of 'a pair of turtledoves or two young pigeons,' in accordance with the dictate in the law of the Lord" (Luke 2:24).

Hail Mary

"Now there was a man in Jerusalem whose name was Simeon... and the holy Spirit was upon him. It had been revealed to him by the holy Spirit that he should not see death before he had seen the Messiah of the Lord" (Luke 2:25–26).

Hail Mary

"He came in the Spirit into the temple; and when the parents brought in the child Jesus to perform the custom of the law in regard to him, he took him into his arms and blessed God, saying:" (Luke 2:27–28).

Hail Mary

"Now, Master, you may let your servant go in peace, according to your word, for my eyes have seen your salvation" (Luke 2:29–30).

Hail Mary

"[The salvation] which you prepared in sight of all the peoples, a light for revelation to the Gentiles, and glory for your people Israel" (Luke 2:31–32).

Hail Mary

"...Simeon blessed them and said to Mary his mother, 'Behold, this child is destined for the fall and rise of many in Israel, and to be a sign that will be contradicted'" (Luke 2:34).

Hail Mary

"(and you yourself a sword will pierce) so that the thoughts of many hearts may be revealed" (Luke 2:35).

Hail Mary

"There was also a prophetess, Anna....She gave thanks to God and spoke about the child to all who were awaiting the redemption of Jerusalem" (Luke 2:36, 38).

Hail Mary

"When they had fulfilled all the prescriptions of the law of the Lord, they returned to Galilee, to their own town of Nazareth. The child grew and became strong, filled with wisdom; and the favor of God was upon him" (Luke 2:39–40).

Hail Mary, Glory Be, Oh my Jesus

The Fifth Joyful Mystery:
Finding of the Child Jesus in the Temple

The fruit of the mystery is joy in finding Jesus.
~ I offer this decade for (say your intention).

Our Father

"Each year his parents went to Jerusalem for the feast of Passover, and when he was twelve years old, they went up according to festival custom" (Luke 2:41–42).

Hail Mary

"After they had completed its days, as they were returning, the boy Jesus remained behind in Jerusalem, but his parents did not know it" (Luke 2:43).

Hail Mary

"Thinking that he was in the caravan, they journeyed for a day and looked for him among their relatives and acquaintances, but not finding him, they returned to Jerusalem to look for him" (Luke 2:44–45).

Hail Mary

"After three days they found him in the temple, sitting in the midst of the teachers, listening to them and asking them questions" (Luke 2:46).

Hail Mary

"And all who heard him were astounded at his understanding and his answers. When his parents saw him, they were astonished" (Luke 2:47–48).

Hail Mary

"...And his mother said to him, 'Son, why have you done this to us? Your father and I have been looking for you with great anxiety'" (Luke 2:48).

Hail Mary

"And he said to them, 'Why were you looking for me? Did you not know that I must be in my Father's house?'" (Luke 2:49).

Hail Mary

"But they did not understand what he said to them. He went down with them and came to Nazareth, and was obedient to them" (Luke 2:50–51).

Hail Mary

"And his mother kept all these things in her heart" (Luke 2:51).

Hail Mary

"And Jesus advanced (in) wisdom and age and favor before God and man" (Luke 2:52).

Hail Mary, Glory Be, Oh my Jesus

Concluding prayers on page 54

THE LUMINOUS MYSTERIES

The First Luminous Mystery:
The Baptism of Jesus

The fruit of the mystery is openness to the Holy Spirit.
~ I offer this decade for (say your intention).

Our Father

"In those days John the Baptist appeared, preaching in the desert of Judea (and) saying, 'Repent, for the kingdom of heaven is at hand!'" (Matthew 3:1–2).

Hail Mary

"It was of him that the prophet Isaiah had spoken when he said: 'A voice of one crying out in the desert, "Prepare the way of the Lord, make straight his paths"'" (Matthew 3:3).

Hail Mary

"At that time Jerusalem, all Judea, and the whole region around the Jordan were going out to him and were being baptized by him in the Jordan River as they acknowledged their sins" (Matthew 3:5–6).

Hail Mary

"I am baptizing you with water, for repentance, but the one who is coming after me is mightier than I. I am not worthy to carry his sandals. He will baptize you with the holy Spirit and fire" (Matthew 3:11).

Hail Mary

"Then Jesus came from Galilee to John at the Jordan to be baptized by him" (Matthew 3:13).

Hail Mary

"John tried to prevent him, saying, 'I need to be baptized by you, and yet you are coming to me?'" (Matthew 3:14).

Hail Mary

Jesus said to him in reply, 'Allow it now, for thus it is fitting for us to fulfill all righteousness.' Then he allowed him" (Matthew 3:15).

Hail Mary

"After Jesus was baptized, he came up from the water and behold, the heavens were opened (for him), and he saw the Spirit of God descending like a dove (and) coming upon him" (Matthew 3:16).

Hail Mary

"And a voice came from the heavens, saying, 'This is my beloved Son, with whom I am well pleased'" (Matthew 3:17).

Hail Mary

"When Jesus began his ministry he was about thirty years of age" (Luke 3:23).

Hail Mary, Glory Be, Oh my Jesus

The Second Luminous Mystery:
The Wedding at Cana

The fruit of the mystery is to Jesus through Mary.
~ I offer this decade for (say your intention).

Our Father

"On the third day there was a wedding in Cana in Galilee, and the mother of Jesus was there" (John 2:1).

Hail Mary

"Jesus and his disciples were also invited to the wedding" (John 2:2).

Hail Mary

"When the wine ran short, the mother of Jesus said to him, 'They have no wine'" (John 2:3).

Hail Mary

"(And) Jesus said to her, 'Woman, how does your concern affect me? My hour has not yet come'" (John 2:4).

Hail Mary

"His mother said to the servers, 'Do whatever he tells you'" (John 2:5).

Hail Mary

"Now there were six stone water jars there for Jewish ceremonial washings, each holding twenty to thirty gallons. Jesus told them, 'Fill the jars with water.' So they filled them to the brim" (John 2:6–7).

Hail Mary

"Then he told them, 'Draw some out now and take it to the headwaiter.' So they took it" (John 2:8).

Hail Mary

"And when the headwaiter tasted the water that had become wine, without knowing where it came from (although the servers who had drawn the water knew)..." (John 2:9).

Hail Mary

"The headwaiter called the bridegroom and said to him, 'Everyone serves good wine first, and then when people have drunk freely, an inferior one; but you have kept the good wine until now'" (John 2:9–10).

Hail Mary

"Jesus did this as the beginning of his signs in Cana in Galilee and so revealed his glory, and his disciples began to believe in him" (John 2:11).

Hail Mary, Glory Be, Oh my Jesus

The Third Luminous Mystery:
The Proclamation of the Kingdom

The fruit of the mystery is repentance and trust in God.
~ I offer this decade for (say your intention).

Our Father

"From that time on, Jesus began to preach and say, 'Repent, for the kingdom of heaven is at hand.' ...He went around all of Galilee, teaching in their synagogues, proclaiming the gospel of the kingdom, and curing every disease and illness among the people" (Matthew 4:17, 23).

Hail Mary

"You shall love the Lord your God with all your heart, with all your soul, with all your mind, and with all your strength. ...'You shall love your neighbor as yourself.' There is no other commandment greater than these" (Mark 12:30–31).

Hail Mary

"But I say to you, love your enemies, and pray for those who persecute you, that you may be children of your heavenly Father" (Matthew 5:44–45).

Hail Mary

"And there people brought to him a paralytic lying on a stretcher. When Jesus saw their faith, he said to the paralytic, 'Courage, child, your sins are forgiven'" (Matthew 9:2).

Hail Mary

"A woman suffering hemorrhages for twelve years came up behind him and touched the tassel on his cloak....Jesus turned around and saw her, and said, 'Courage, daughter! Your faith has saved you'" (Matthew 9:20, 22).

Hail Mary

"Then Peter approaching asked him, 'Lord, if my brother sins against me, how often must I forgive him? As many as seven times?' Jesus answered, 'I say to you, not seven times but seventy-seven times'" (Matthew 18:21–22).

Hail Mary

"Stop judging and you will not be judged. Stop condemning and you will not be condemned. Forgive and you will be forgiven" (Luke 6:37).

Hail Mary

"The kingdom of heaven is like a mustard seed that a person took and sowed in a field. It is the smallest of all the seeds, yet when full-grown it is the largest of plants. It becomes a large bush, and the 'birds of the sky come and dwell in its branches'" (Matthew 13:31–32).

Hail Mary

"The kingdom of heaven is like a treasure buried in a field, which a person finds and hides again, and out of joy goes and sells all that he has and buys that field" (Matthew 13:44).

Hail Mary

"Jesus spoke to them again, saying, 'I am the light of the world. Whoever follows me will not walk in darkness, but will have the light of life'" (John 8:12).

Hail Mary, Glory Be, Oh my Jesus

The Fourth Luminous Mystery:
The Transfiguration

The fruit of the mystery is desire of holiness.
~ I offer this decade for (say your intention).

Our Father

"After six days Jesus took Peter, James, and John his brother, and led them up a high mountain by themselves" (Matthew 17:1).

Hail Mary

"...He was transfigured before them; his face shone like the sun and his clothes became white as light" (Matthew 17:2).

Hail Mary

"And behold, Moses and Elijah appeared to them, conversing with him" (Matthew 17:3).

Hail Mary

"Then Peter said to Jesus in reply, 'Lord, it is good that we are here'" (Matthew 17:4).

Hail Mary

"'If you wish, I will make three tents here, one for you, one for Moses, and one for Elijah'" (Matthew 17:4).

Hail Mary

"While he was still speaking, behold, a bright cloud cast a shadow over them, then from the cloud came a voice that said..." (Matthew 17:5).

Hail Mary

"...This is my beloved Son, with whom I am well pleased; listen to him" (Matthew 17:5).

Hail Mary

"When the disciples heard this, they fell prostrate and were very much afraid" (Matthew 17:6).

Hail Mary

"But Jesus came and touched them, saying, 'Rise, and do not be afraid.' And when the disciples raised their eyes, they saw no one else but Jesus alone" (Matthew 17:7–8).

Hail Mary

"As they were coming down from the mountain, Jesus charged them, 'Do not tell the vision to anyone until the Son of Man has been raised from the dead'" (Matthew 17:9).

Hail Mary, Glory Be, Oh my Jesus

The Fifth Luminous Mystery:
The Institution of the Eucharist

The fruit of the mystery is adoration.

~ I offer this decade for (say your intention).

Our Father

"When the day of the Feast of Unleavened Bread arrived...he sent out Peter and John, instructing them, 'Go and make preparations for us to eat the Passover'" (Luke 22:7–8).

Hail Mary

"They asked him, 'Where do you want us to make the preparations?'" (Luke 22:9).

Hail Mary

"[Jesus] said, 'Go into the city to a certain man and tell him, "The teacher says, 'My appointed time draws near; in your house I shall celebrate the Passover with my disciples'"'" (Matthew 26:18).

Hail Mary

"He will show you a large upper room that is furnished. Make preparations there" (Luke 22:12).

Hail Mary

"Then they went off and found everything exactly as he had told them, and there they prepared the Passover. When the hour came, he took his place at table with the apostles" (Luke 22:13–14).

Hail Mary

"[Jesus] took the bread, said the blessing, broke it, and gave it to them, saying, 'This is my body, which will be given for you; do this in memory of me'" (Luke 22:19).

Hail Mary

"Then he took a cup, gave thanks, and gave it to them, saying..." (Matthew 26:27).

Hail Mary

"...Drink from it, all of you, for this is my blood of the covenant, which will be shed on behalf of many for the forgiveness of sins" (Matthew 26:27–28).

Hail Mary

"I tell you, from now on I shall not drink this fruit of the vine until the day when I drink it with you new in the kingdom of my Father" (Matthew 26:29).

Hail Mary

"Jesus said to them,...'Whoever eats my flesh and drinks my blood has eternal life, and I will raise him on the last day. For my flesh is true food, and my blood is true drink. Whoever eats my flesh and drinks my blood remains in me and I in him'" (John 6:53–56).

Hail Mary, Glory Be, Oh my Jesus

Concluding prayers on page 54

THE SORROWFUL MYSTERIES

The First Sorrowful Mystery:
The Agony in the Garden

The fruit of the mystery is sorrow for sin.

~ I offer this decade for (say your intention).

Our Father

"Then Jesus came with them to a place called Gethsemane, and he said to his disciples, 'Sit here while I go over there and pray.'... and [he] began to feel sorrow and distress" (Matthew 26:36–37).

Hail Mary

"Then he said to them, 'My soul is sorrowful even to death. Remain here and keep watch with me'" (Matthew 26:38).

Hail Mary

"After withdrawing about a stone's throw from them and kneeling, he prayed..." (Luke 22:41).

Hail Mary

"...Saying, 'Father, if it is possible, let this cup pass from me; yet, not as I will, but as you will'" (Matthew 26:39).

Hail Mary

"And to strengthen him an angel from heaven appeared to him. He was in such agony and he prayed so fervently that his sweat became like drops of blood falling on the ground" (Luke 22:43–44).

Hail Mary

"When he returned to his disciples he found them asleep. He said to Peter, 'So you could not keep watch with me for one hour? Watch and pray that you may not undergo the test. The spirit is willing, but the flesh is weak'" (Matthew 26:40–41).

Hail Mary

"Behold, the hour is at hand when the Son of Man is to be handed over to sinners. Get up, let us go. Look, my betrayer is at hand" (Matthew 26:45–46).

Hail Mary

"While he was still speaking, Judas, one of the Twelve, arrived, accompanied by a large crowd, with swords and clubs" (Matthew 26:47).

Hail Mary

"Immediately he went over to Jesus and said, 'Hail, Rabbi!' and he kissed him" (Matthew 26:49).

Hail Mary

"Jesus answered him, 'My friend, do what you have come for.' Then stepping forward they laid hands on Jesus and arrested him" (Matthew 26:50).

Hail Mary, Glory Be, Oh my Jesus

The Second Sorrowful Mystery:
The Scouring at the Pillar

The fruit of the mystery is purity.

~ I offer this decade for (say your intention).

Our Father

"As soon as morning came, the chief priests with the elders and the scribes...held a council. They bound Jesus, led him away, and handed him over to Pilate" (Mark 15:1).

Hail Mary

"Pilate questioned him, 'Are you the king of the Jews?' Jesus answered, 'My kingdom does not belong to this world'" (Mark 15:2, John 18:36).

Hail Mary

"So Pilate said to him, 'Then you are a king?' Jesus answered, 'You say I am a king'" (John 18:37).

Hail Mary

"For this I was born and for this I came into the world, to testify to the truth. Everyone who belongs to the truth listens to my voice" (John 18:37).

Hail Mary

"Pilate said to him, 'What is truth?' When he had said this, he again went out to the Jews and said to them, 'I find no guilt in him'" (John 18:38).

Hail Mary

"'Therefore, I shall have him flogged and then release him.' Then Pilate took Jesus and had him scourged" (Luke 23:16, John 19:1).

Hail Mary

"The men who held Jesus in custody were ridiculing and beating him. They blindfolded him and questioned him, saying..." (Luke 22:63–64).

Hail Mary

"'...Prophesy! Who is it that struck you?' And they reviled him in saying many other things against him" (Luke 22:64–65).

Hail Mary

"I gave my back to those who beat me, my cheeks to those who tore out my beard; My face I did not hide from insults and spitting" (Isaiah 50:6).

Hail Mary

"I have become a laughingstock to all my people, their taunt all day long" (Lamentations 3:14).

Hail Mary, Glory Be, Oh my Jesus

The Third Sorrowful Mystery:
The Crowning of Thorns

The fruit of the mystery is courage.
~ I offer this decade for (say your intention).

Our Father

"The soldiers led him away inside the palace, that is, the praetorium, and assembled the whole cohort" (Mark 15:16).

Hail Mary

"They clothed him in purple and, weaving a crown of thorns, placed it on him" (Mark 15:17).

Hail Mary

"They began to salute him with, 'Hail, King of the Jews!'" (Mark 15:18).

Hail Mary

"And [they] kept striking his head with a reed and spitting upon him. They knelt before him in homage" (Mark 15:19).

Hail Mary

"Once more Pilate went out and said to them, 'Look, I am bringing him out to you, so that you may know that I find no guilt in him'" (John 19:4).

Hail Mary

"So Jesus came out, wearing the crown of thorns and the purple cloak. And he said to them, 'Behold, the man!'" (John 19:5).

Hail Mary

"When the chief priests and the guards saw him they cried out, 'Crucify him, Crucify him!'" (John 19:6).

Hail Mary

"Pilate said to them, 'Why? What evil has he done?' They only shouted the louder, 'Crucify him'" (Mark 15:14).

Hail Mary

"And [Pilate] said to the Jews, 'Behold, your king!' They cried out, 'Take him away, take him away! Crucify him!' Pilate said to them, 'Shall I crucify your king?' The chief priests answered, 'We have no king but Caesar'" (John 19:14–15).

Hail Mary

"Then [Pilate] handed him over to them to be crucified" (John 19:16).

Hail Mary, Glory Be, Oh my Jesus

The Fourth Sorrowful Mystery:
The Carrying of the Cross

The fruit of the mystery is patience.

~ I offer this decade for (say your intention).

Our Father

"When they had mocked him, they stripped him of the cloak, dressed him in his own clothes, and led him off to crucify him" (Matthew 27:31).

Hail Mary

"As they were going out, they met a Cyrenian named Simon; this man they pressed into service to carry his cross" (Matthew 27:32).

Hail Mary

"A large crowd of people followed Jesus, including many women who mourned and lamented him" (Luke 23:27).

Hail Mary

"Jesus turned to them and said, 'Daughters of Jerusalem, do not weep for me; weep instead for yourselves and for your children'" (Luke 23:28).

Hail Mary

"Now two others, both criminals, were led away with him to be executed" (Luke 23:32).

Hail Mary

"And when they came to a place called Golgotha (which means Place of the Skull), they gave Jesus wine to drink mixed with gall. But when he tasted it, he refused to drink" (Matthew 27:33–34).

Hail Mary

"After they had crucified him, they divided his garments by casting lots; then they sat down and kept watch over him there" (Matthew 27:35–36).

Hail Mary

"If anyone wishes to come after me, he must deny himself..." (Luke 9:23).

Hail Mary

"...and take up his cross daily and follow me" (Luke 9:23).

Hail Mary

"For whoever wishes to save his life will lose it, but whoever loses his life for my sake will save it" (Luke 9:24).

Hail Mary, Glory Be, Oh my Jesus

The Fifth Sorrowful Mystery: The Crucifixion

The fruit of the mystery is perseverance.
~ I offer this decade for (say your intention).

Our Father

"...Jesus said, 'Father, forgive them, they know not what they do'" (Luke 23:34).

Hail Mary

"[One of the criminals] said, 'Jesus, remember me when you come into your kingdom.' [Jesus] replied to him, 'Amen, I say to you, today you will be with me in Paradise'" (Luke 23:42–43).

Hail Mary

"When Jesus saw his mother and the disciple there whom he loved, he said to his mother, 'Woman, behold, your son'" (John 19:26).

Hail Mary

"Then he said to the disciple, 'Behold, your mother.' And from that hour the disciple took her into his home" (John 19:27).

Hail Mary

"And about three o'clock Jesus cried out in a loud voice, *'Eli, Eli, lema sabachthani?'* which means, 'My God, my God, why have you forsaken me?'" (Matthew 27:46).

Hail Mary

"After this, aware that everything was now finished, in order that the scripture might be fulfilled, Jesus said, 'I thirst'" (John 19:28).

Hail Mary

"There was a vessel filled with common wine. So they put a sponge soaked in wine on a sprig of hyssop and put it up to his mouth. When Jesus had taken the wine, he said, 'It is finished'" (John 19:29–30).

Hail Mary

"It was now about noon and darkness came over the whole land until three in the afternoon because of an eclipse of the sun. Then the veil of the temple was torn down the middle" (Luke 23:44–45).

Hail Mary

"Jesus cried out in a loud voice, 'Father, into your hands I commend my spirit'; and when he had said this he breathed his last" (Luke 23:46).

Hail Mary

"...When they came to Jesus and saw that he was already dead, they did not break his legs, but one soldier thrust his lance into his side, and immediately blood and water flowed out" (John 19:33–34).

Hail Mary, Glory Be, Oh my Jesus

Concluding prayers on page 54

THE GLORIOUS MYSTERIES

The First Glorious Mystery:
The Resurrection

The fruit of the mystery is faith.

~ I offer this decade for (say your intention).

Our Father

"When the sabbath was over, Mary Magdalene, Mary, the mother of James, and Salome bought spices so that they might go and anoint him. Very early when the sun had risen, on the first day of the week, they came to the tomb" (Mark 16:1–2).

Hail Mary

"They were saying to one another, 'Who will roll back the stone for us from the entrance to the tomb?' When they looked up, they saw that the stone had been rolled back; it was very large" (Mark 16:3–4).

Hail Mary

"On entering the tomb they saw a young man sitting on the right side, clothed in a white robe, and they were utterly amazed. He said to them, 'Do not be amazed!'" (Mark 16:5–6).

Hail Mary

"You seek Jesus of Nazareth, the crucified. He has been raised; he is not here. Behold the place where they laid him" (Mark 16:6).

Hail Mary

"'But go and tell his disciples and Peter, "He is going before you to Galilee; there you will see him, as he told you."' Then [the women] went out and fled from the tomb" (Mark 16:7–8).

Hail Mary

"...That very day two of them were going to a village seven miles from Jerusalem called Emmaus, and they were conversing about all the things that had occurred. And it happened that while they were conversing and debating, Jesus himself drew near and walked with them, but their eyes were prevented from recognizing him" (Luke 24:13–16).

Hail Mary

"Then beginning with Moses and all the prophets, he interpreted to them what referred to him in all the scriptures. ...And it happened that, while he was with them at table, he took bread, said the blessing, broke it, and gave it to them. With that their eyes were opened and they recognized him" (Luke 24:27, 30–31).

Hail Mary

"On the evening of that first day of the week, when the doors were locked, where the disciples were, for fear of the Jews, Jesus came and stood in their midst and said to them, 'Peace be with you'" (John 20:19).

Hail Mary

"When he had said this, he showed them his hands and his side. The disciples rejoiced when they saw the Lord. [Jesus] said to them again, 'Peace be with you'" (John 20:20–21).

Hail Mary

"I am the resurrection and the life; whoever believes in me, even if he dies, will live, and everyone who lives and believes in me will never die" (John 11:25–26).

Hail Mary, Glory Be, Oh my Jesus

The Second Glorious Mystery:
The Ascension

The fruit of the mystery is hope.
~ I offer this decade for (say your intention).

Our Father

"Then [Jesus] led them (out) as far as Bethany, raised his hands, and blessed them" (Luke 24:50).

Hail Mary

"...Jesus approached and said to them, 'All power in heaven and on earth has been given to me'" (Matthew 28:18).

Hail Mary

"Go, therefore, and make disciples of all nations, baptizing them in the name of the Father, and of the Son, and of the holy Spirit..." (Matthew 28:19).

Hail Mary

"...teaching them to observe all that I have commanded you" (Matthew 28:20).

Hail Mary

"And behold, I am with you always, until the end of the age" (Matthew 28:20).

Hail Mary

"Whoever believes and is baptized will be saved..." (Mark 16:16).

Hail Mary

"Whoever does not believe will be condemned" (Mark 16:16).

Hail Mary

"As [Jesus] blessed them he parted from them and was taken up to heaven" (Luke 24:51).

Hail Mary

"They did him homage and then returned to Jerusalem with great joy" (Luke 24:52).

Hail Mary

"Jesus...took his seat at the right hand of God" (Mark 16:19).

Hail Mary, Glory Be, Oh my Jesus

The Third Glorious Mystery:
The Descent of the Holy Spirit

The fruit of the mystery is Love of God.
~ I offer this decade for (say your intention).

Our Father

"When they entered the city they went to the upper room where they were staying" (Acts 1:13).

Hail Mary

"All these devoted themselves with one accord to prayer, together with some women, and Mary the mother of Jesus" (Acts 1:14).

Hail Mary

"When the time for Pentecost was fulfilled, they were all in one place together" (Acts 2:1).

Hail Mary

"And suddenly there came from the sky a noise like a strong driving wind, and it filled the entire house in which they were" (Acts 2:2).

Hail Mary

"Then there appeared to them tongues as of fire, which parted and came to rest on each one of them" (Acts 2:3).

Hail Mary

"And they were all filled with the holy Spirit, and began to speak in different tongues, as the Spirit enabled them to proclaim" (Acts 2:4).

Hail Mary

"Now there were devout Jews staying in Jerusalem. At this sound, they gathered in a large crowd, but they were confused because each one heard them speaking in his own language" (Acts 2:5–6).

Hail Mary

"Then Peter stood up with the Eleven, raised his voice, and proclaimed to them..." (Acts 2:14).

Hail Mary

"Repent and be baptized, every one of you, in the name of Jesus Christ for the forgiveness of your sins; and you will receive the gift of the holy Spirit" (Acts 2:38).

Hail Mary

"Those who accepted his message were baptized, and about three thousand persons were added that day" (Acts 2:41).

Hail Mary, Glory Be, Oh my Jesus

The Fourth Glorious Mystery:
The Assumption

The fruit of the mystery is the grace of a Holy Death.

~ I offer this decade for (say your intention).

Our Father

"Come then, my love, my lovely one, come" (Song of Solomon 2:10, from the *Jerusalem Bible*).

Hail Mary

"For see, the winter is past, the rains are over and gone" (Song of Solomon 2:11, from the *Jerusalem Bible*).

Hail Mary

"You are all beautiful, my love, and without a blemish" (Song of Solomon 4:7, from the *Jerusalem Bible*).

Hail Mary

"All glorious is the king's daughter as she enters, her raiment threaded with gold" (Psalm 45:14).

Hail Mary

"In embroidered apparel she is led to the king" (Psalm 45:15).

Hail Mary

"I will rejoice heartily in the LORD, my being exults in my God; for he has clothed me with garments of salvation, and wrapped me in a robe of justice...as a bride adorns herself with her jewels" (Isaiah 61:10).

Hail Mary

"I will sing of your mercy forever, LORD proclaim your faithfulness through all ages" (Psalm 89:2).

Hail Mary

"Amen, Blessing and glory, wisdom and thanksgiving, honor, power, and might be to our God forever and ever. Amen" (Revelation 7:12).

Hail Mary

"Death is swallowed up in victory.
Where, O death, is your victory?
Where, O death, is your sting?" (1 Corinthians 15:54–55).

Hail Mary

"O Mary, Mother of grace and Mother of Mercy, do thou protect me from the enemy, and receive me at the hour of my death" (the *Raccolta*, No. 307).

Hail Mary, Glory Be, Oh my Jesus

The Fifth Glorious Mystery:
The Coronation

The fruit of the mystery is Trust in Mary's Intercession.
~ I offer this decade for (say your intention).

Our Father

"Remain faithful until death, and I will give you the crown of life" (Revelation 2:10).

Hail Mary

"Then God's temple in heaven was opened, and the ark of his covenant could be seen in the temple" (Revelation 11:19).

Hail Mary

"A great sign appeared in the sky, a woman clothed with the sun, with the moon under her feet, and on her head a crown of twelve stars" (Revelation 12:1–2).

Hail Mary

"May you be blessed, my daughter by God Most High, beyond all women on earth" (Judith 13:18, from the *Jerusalem Bible*).

Hail Mary

"The trust you have shown shall not pass from the memories of men, but shall ever remind them of the power of God" (Judith 13:19, from the *Jerusalem Bible*).

Hail Mary

"You are the glory of Jerusalem! You are the great pride of Israel! You are the highest honor of our race!" (Judith 15:9, from the *Jerusalem Bible*).

Hail Mary

"My throne in a pillar of cloud and for eternity I shall remain" (Ecclesiasticus 24:4, 9, from the *Jerusalem Bible*).

Hail Mary

"I am the rose of Sharon, the lily of the valleys" (Song of Solomon 2:1, from the *Jerusalem Bible*).

Hail Mary

"Behold, from now on will all ages call me blessed. The Mighty One has done great things for me, and holy is his name" (Luke 1:48–49).

Hail Mary

"O Mary, my Queen and my Mother. Remember I am all thine. Keep me and guard me as thy property and possession" (Short form of consecration).

Hail Mary, Glory Be, Oh my Jesus

CONCLUDING PRAYERS

The Hail Holy Queen (The Salve Regina)

Hail, holy Queen, mother of mercy,
our life, our sweetness, and our hope.
To you we cry, poor banished children of Eve;
to you we send up our sighs,
mourning and weeping in this valley of tears.
Turn, then, most gracious advocate,
your eyes of mercy toward us;
and after this, our exile,
show unto us the blessed fruit of your womb, Jesus.
O clement, O loving, O sweet Virgin Mary.

Let Us Pray

O God, whose only begotten Son by his life, Death and Resurrection has purchased for us the rewards of eternal life, grant, we beseech Thee, that meditating on these mysteries of the most holy rosary of the Blessed Virgin Mary, we may imitate what they contain and obtain what they promise, through the same Christ our Lord. Amen.

*Pray one Our Father, one Hail Mary,
and one Glory Be for the intentions of the pope.*

OPTIONAL PRAYERS

O Sacrament most holy. O Sacrament divine.
All praise and all thanksgiving be every moment Thine.

Prayer to St. Michael the Archangel (page 102)

Prayer to Your Guardian Angel (page 102)

St. Joseph Prayer After the Rosary

Glorious St. Joseph, spouse of the Immaculate Virgin, obtain for me and all the members of my family and loved ones, a confident, sinless, generous, and patient heart, and perfect resignation to the Divine Will. Be our guide, father, and model throughout life, that we may merit a death like yours, in the arms of Jesus and Mary. Amen.

Come Holy Spirit by the Powerful Intercession

Come Holy Spirit! Come by means of the powerful intercession of the Immaculate Heart of Mary your well Beloved Spouse!

May the Divine Assistance Remain Always With Us

May the Divine Assistance remain always with us, and may the souls of the faithful departed, through the mercy of God, rest in peace. Amen.

The Litany of Loreto

Lord, have mercy.
   Lord, have mercy.
Christ, have mercy.
   Christ, have mercy.
Lord, have mercy.
   Lord, have mercy.

God our Father in Heaven,
   have mercy on us.
God the Son, Redeemer of the world,
   have mercy on us.
God the Holy Spirit,
   have mercy on us.
Holy Trinity, one God,
   have mercy on us.

Holy Mary,
   pray for us. (Say this after each phrase.)
Holy Mother of God,
Most honored of virgins,
Mother of Christ,
Mother of the Church,
Mother of Divine grace,
Mother most pure,
Mother of chaste love,
Mother and virgin,
Sinless Mother,
Dearest of mothers,
Model of motherhood,

Mother of good counsel,
Mother of our Creator,
Mother of our Savior,

Virgin most wise,
Virgin rightly praised,
Virgin rightly renowned,
Virgin most powerful,
Virgin gentle in mercy,

Faithful Virgin,
Mirror of justice,
Throne of wisdom,
Cause of our joy,
Shrine of the Spirit,

Glory of Israel,
Vessel of selfless devotion,
Mystical Rose,
Tower of David,
Tower of ivory,
House of gold,
Ark of the covenant,
Gate of heaven,
Morning Star,
Health of the Sick,
Refuge of sinners,
Comfort of the troubled,
Help of Christians,

Queen of angels,
Queen of patriarchs and prophets,
Queen of apostles and martyrs,
Queen of confessors and virgins,
Queen of all saints,
Queen conceived without original sin,
Queen assumed into heaven,
Queen of the rosary,
Queen of peace,

Lamb of God, you take away the sins of the world;
have mercy on us.
Lamb of God, you take away the sins of the world;
have mercy on us.
Lamb of God, you take away the sins of the world;
have mercy on us.

Pray for us, O holy Mother of God.
That we may become worthy of the promises of Christ.

Let us pray.

Eternal God, let your people enjoy constant health in mind and body. Through the intercession of the Virgin Mary free us from the sorrows of this life and lead us to happiness in the life to come. Grant this through Christ our Lord. Amen.

THE STATIONS OF THE CROSS

*May the Passion of Christ
be always in our hearts.*

MOTTO OF THE PASSIONISTS

The Stations of the Cross, sometimes known as the Way of the Cross or *Via Dolorosa* is a Catholic devotion which remembers the passion and death of our Lord Jesus Christ. There are fourteen stations and each station represents an event which occurred during Jesus' passion and death at Calvary on Good Friday. The Stations of the Cross are found on the walls of almost all Catholic churches. They can be found as paintings or carved images made out of wood or ceramic. The Church's tradition has been to pray the Stations of the Cross during all the Fridays of the holy season of Lent but as a personal devotion can be prayed at any time during the year. To quote an explanation on the Stations from the Diocese of Palm Beach, "Moreover, the great saints all affirm that meditation of the passion and death of Our Savior is the most fruitful that one can engage in."

EXCERPT FROM BLESSED POPE JOHN PAUL II'S OPENING MEDITATION AND PRAYERS

Stations of the Cross at the Colosseum, Good Friday, April 21, 2000

"Whoever wishes to come after me must deny himself, take up his cross, and follow me" (Matthew 16:24).

[Good Friday evening]

For twenty centuries the Church has gathered on this evening to remember and to re-live the events of the final stage of the earthly journey of the Son of God. Once again this year the Church in Rome meets at the Colosseum, to follow the footsteps of Jesus, who "went out, carrying his cross, to the place called the place of the skull, which is called in Hebrew Golgotha" (John 19:17). We are here because we are convinced that the Way of the Cross of the Son of God was not simply a journey to the place of execution. We believe that every step of the Condemned Christ, every action and every word, as well as everything felt and done by those who took part in this tragic drama, continues to speak to us. In his suffering and death too, Christ reveals to us the truth about God and man.

In this Jubilee Year we want to concentrate on the full meaning of that event, so that what happened may speak with new power to our minds and hearts, and become the source of the grace of a real sharing in it. To share means to have a part.

What does it mean to have a part in the cross of Christ? It means to experience, in the Holy Spirit, the love hidden within the cross of Christ. It means to recognize, in the light of this love, our own cross. It means to take up that cross once more and, strengthened by this love, to continue our journey...

To journey through life, in imitation of the one who "endured the cross, despising the shame, and is seated at the right hand of the throne of God" (Hebrews 12:12).

Let us pray.

Lord Jesus Christ, fill our hearts with the light of your Spirit, so that by following you on your final journey we may come to know the price of our Redemption and become worthy of a share in the fruits of your Passion, Death and Resurrection. You who live and reign for ever and ever. Amen.

THE WAY OF THE CROSS

At the cross her station keeping
stood the mournful Mother weeping
close to Jesus to the last.

The First Station:
Jesus Is Condemned to Death

We adore You, O Christ and we praise you.
Because by Your holy cross you have redeemed the world.

"Pilate said to them, 'Then what shall I do with Jesus called Messiah?' They all said, 'Let him be crucified!' But he said, 'Why? What evil has he done?' They only shouted the louder, 'Let him be crucified!' ...After he had Jesus scourged, he handed him over to be crucified" (Matthew 27:22–23, 26).

O Jesus, my Sovereign Good, when Thou wert scourged, what were the sentiments of Thy Most holy Heart! O dear Spouse of my soul, how greatly did the sight of my sins and my ingratitude afflict Thee! O my Love! Would that I could die for Thee!

ST. PAUL OF THE CROSS (1694–1775)

Hail Mary, Glory Be, Oh my Jesus

Christ Jesus crucified, have mercy on us.

Through her heart his sorrow sharing
all his bitter anguish bearing
now at length the sword has passed.

The Second Station:
Jesus Takes Up His Cross

We adore You, O Christ and we praise you.
Because by Your holy cross you have redeemed the world.

"And when they had mocked him, they stripped him of the cloak, dressed him in his own clothes, and led him off to crucify him" (Matthew 27:31).

O my Jesus, I cannot be Thy friend and follower, if I refuse to carry the cross. O dearly beloved cross! I embrace thee, I kiss thee, I joyfully accept thee from the hands of my God. Far be it from me to glory in anything, save in the cross of my Lord and Redeemer. By it the world shall be crucified to me and I to the world, that I may be Thine forever.

ST. FRANCIS OF ASSISI (1182–1226)

Hail Mary, Glory Be, Oh my Jesus

Christ Jesus crucified, have mercy on us.
O, how sad and sore distressed
was that Mother highly blessed
of the sole Begotten One.

The Third Station:
Jesus Falls for the First Time

We adore You, O Christ and we praise you.
Because by Your holy cross you have redeemed the world.

"He was spurned and avoided by men, a man of suffering, knowing pain. Like one from whom you turn your face, spurned, and we held him in no esteem. Yet it was our pain that he bore, our sufferings he endured. We thought of him as stricken, struck down by God and afflicted" (Isaiah 53:3–4).

O Jesus, who in thy bitter Passion didst, become "the reproach of men, and the man of sorrows," I venerate Thy Holy Face on which shone the beauty and gentleness of Divinity. In those disfigured features I recognize Thine infinite love, and I long to love Thee and to make Thee loved.

ST. THÉRÈSE OF LISIEUX (1873–1897)

Our Father, Hail Mary, Glory Be

Christ Jesus crucified, have mercy on us.

Is there one who would not weep,
whelmed in miseries so deep
Christ's dear Mother to behold?

The Fourth Station:
Jesus Meets His Sorrowful Mother

We adore You, O Christ and we praise you.
Because by Your holy cross you have redeemed the world.

"Simeon blessed them and said to Mary his Mother, 'Behold, this child is destined for the fall and rise of many in Israel, and to be a sign that will be contradicted (and you yourself a sword will pierce) so that the thoughts of many hearts will be revealed'" (Luke 2:34–35).

O most sorrowful Mother! Thy heart was pierced with a sword of grief when Simeon foretold to Thee in the Temple of the ignominious death and the desolation of thy divine and most dear Son, which Thou wert destined one day to witness. By the great anguish of thy suffering heart, O gracious Queen of the universe, impress upon my mind, in life and in death, the Sacred Passion of Jesus and thine own sorrows.

ST. ALPHONSUS LIGUORI (1696–1787)

Our Father, Hail Mary, Glory Be

Christ Jesus crucified, have mercy on us.

*Can the human heart refrain
from partaking in her pain
in that Mother's pain untold?*

The Fifth Station:
Simon of Cyrene Helps Jesus Carry His Cross

We adore You, O Christ and we praise you.
Because by Your holy cross you have redeemed the world.

"As they led him away they took hold of a certain Simon, a Cyrenian, who was coming in from the country; and after laying the cross on him, they made him carry it behind Jesus" (Luke 23:26).

My Saviour! I cheerfully accept all the painful dispositions, in which it is Thy pleasure to place me. My wish is in all things to conform myself to Thy holy will. Whenever I kiss Thy cross, it is to show that I submit perfectly to mine.

ST. MARGARET MARY ALACOQUE (1647–1690)

Our Father, Hail Mary, Glory Be

Christ Jesus crucified, have mercy on us.

*Let me share with thee His pain
who for all my sins was slain,
who for me in torments died.*

The Sixth Station:
Veronica Wipes the Face of Jesus

We adore You, O Christ and we praise you.
Because by Your holy cross you have redeemed the world.

"'Lord, when did we see you hungry, and feed you, or thirsty and give you drink? When did we see you a stranger and welcome you, or naked and clothe you? When did we see you ill or in prison, and visit you?' And the king will say to them in reply, 'Amen, I say to you, whatever you did for one of these least brothers of mine, you did for me'" (Matthew 25:37–40).

Make us worthy, Lord, to serve those people throughout the world who live and die in poverty and hunger. Give them through our hands, this day, their daily bread, and by our understanding love, give them peace and joy.

BLESSED MOTHER TERESA OF CALCUTTA (1910–1997)

Our Father, Hail Mary, Glory Be

Christ Jesus crucified, have mercy on us.

Let me mingle tears with thee,
mourning Him who mourned for me
all the days that I may live.

The Seventh Station:
Jesus Falls for the Second Time

We adore You, O Christ and we praise you.
Because by Your holy cross you have redeemed the world.

"But he was pierced for our sins, crushed for our iniquity. He bore the punishment that makes us whole, by his wounds we were healed. We had all gone astray like sheep, all following our own way; But the LORD laid upon him the guilt of us all" (Isaiah 53:5–6).

Oh my Jesus, clasp me tenderly, firmly, close to You that I may never leave You alone in Your cruel Passion. I ask only for a place of rest in Your heart. My desire is to share in Your agony and be beside You....May my soul be inebriated by Your love and fed with the bread of Your sorrow.

ST. PADRE PIO (1887–1968)

Our Father, Hail Mary, Glory Be

Christ Jesus crucified, have mercy on us.

Make me feel as thou hast felt;
make my soul to glow and melt
with the love of Christ my Lord.

The Eighth Station:
Jesus Meets the Women of Jerusalem

We adore You, O Christ and we praise you.
Because by Your holy cross you have redeemed the world.

"A large crowd of people followed Jesus, including many women who mourned and lamented him. Jesus turned to them and said, 'Daughters of Jerusalem, do not weep for me; weep instead for yourselves and for your children'" (Luke 23:27–28).

Precious Blood, ocean of Divine Mercy: Flow upon us!
Precious Blood, most pure offering: Procure us every grace!
Precious Blood, hope and refuge of sinners: Atone for us!
Precious Blood, delight of holy souls: Draw us!

ST. CATHERINE OF SIENA (1347–1380)

Our Father, Hail Mary, Glory Be

Christ Jesus crucified, have mercy on us.

O thou Mother! Fount of love!
touch my spirit from above,
make my heart with thine accord.

The Ninth Station:
Jesus Falls for the Third Time

We adore You of Christ and we praise you.
Because by Your holy cross you have redeemed the world.

"Though harshly treated, he submitted and did not open his mouth; Like a lamb led to slaughter or a sheep silent before shearers, he did not open his mouth. He was given a grave among the wicked, a burial place with evildoers. Though he had done no wrong, nor was deceit found in his mouth" (Isaiah 53:7, 9).

My Jesus, give me a great devotion to Thy most holy passion, that Thy pains and Thy death may be always before my eyes, to inflame me always with love for Thee, and to incite me always to make some return of gratitude for so much love.

ST. FRANCIS DE SALES (1567–1622)

Our Father, Hail Mary, Glory Be

Christ Jesus crucified, have mercy on us.

Wounded with His ev'ry wound
steep my soul till it hath swooned
in His very Blood away.

The Tenth Station:
Jesus Is Stripped of His Garments

We adore You, O Christ and we praise you.
Because by Your holy cross you have redeemed the world.

"When the soldiers had crucified Jesus, they took his clothes and divided them into four shares, a share for each soldier. They also took his tunic, but the tunic was seamless, woven in one piece from the top down. So they said to one another, 'Let's not tear it, but cast lots for it to see whose it will be," in order that the passage of Scripture might be fulfilled (that says): They divided my garments among them, and for my vesture they cast lots'" (John 19:23–24).

Why did you suffer for me, dear Jesus? For love! The nails...the crown...the cross...all for love of me! For You, I sacrifice everything willingly. I offer You my body with all its weakness, and my soul with all its love....Do not abandon me, Jesus I am yours.

ST. GEMMA GALGANI (1878–1903)

Our Father, Hail Mary, Glory Be

Christ Jesus crucified, have mercy on us.

Bruised, derided, cursed, defiled,
she beheld her tender Child
all with bloody scourges rent.

The Eleventh Station:
Jesus Is Nailed to the Cross

We adore You, O Christ and we praise you.
Because by Your holy cross you have redeemed the world.

"When they came to the place called the Skull, they crucified him and the criminals there, one on his right and the other on his left. (Then Jesus said, 'Father, forgive them, they know not what they do')" (Luke 23:33–34).

Lord Jesus Christ, who stretched out your hands on the cross and redeemed us by Your Blood: forgive me, a sinner for none of my thoughts are hidden from you. Pardon I seek, pardon I hope for, pardon I trust to have. You who are full of pity and mercy: spare me and forgive me.

ST. AMBROSE (340–397)

Our Father, Hail Mary, Glory Be

Christ Jesus crucified, have mercy on us.

Holy Mother! Pierce me through;
in my heart each wound renew
of my Savior crucified.

The Twelfth Station:
Jesus Dies on the Cross

We adore You, O Christ and we praise you.
Because by Your holy cross you have redeemed the world.

"It was now about noon and darkness came over the whole land until three in the afternoon....Jesus cried out in a loud voice, 'Father, into your hands I commend my spirit,' and when he had said this he breathed his last. When they came to Jesus and saw that he was already dead, they did not break his legs, but one soldier thrust his lance into his side, and immediately blood and water flowed out" (Luke 23:44–46, John 19:33–34).

You expired, Jesus, but the source of life gushed forth for souls, and the ocean of mercy opened up for the whole world. O Fount of Life, unfathomable Divine Mercy, envelop the whole world and empty Yourself out upon us (Diary of St. Maria Faustina Kowalska, 1319). O Blood and Water, which gushed forth from the Heart of Jesus as a Fount of Mercy for us, I trust in You! (Diary of St. Maria Faustina Kowalska, 186)

ST. FAUSTINA (1905–1938)

Our Father, Hail Mary, Glory Be

> *Christ Jesus crucified, have mercy on us.*

> *For the sins of His own nation,*
> *saw Him hang in desolation*
> *till His Spirit forth He sent.*

The Thirteenth Station:
Jesus Is Taken Down From the Cross

We adore You, O Christ and we praise you.
Because by Your holy cross you have redeemed the world.

"Joseph of Arimathea, secretly a disciple of Jesus for fear of the Jews, asked Pilate if he could remove the body of Jesus. And Pilate permitted it. So he came and took his body" (John 19:38).

Praise and glory be to you, O loving Jesus Christ, for the most sacred wound in your side...and for your infinite mercy which you made known to us. And, by your most bitter death, give me a lively faith, a firm hope, and a perfect charity, so that I may love you with all my heart and all my soul, and all my strength.

ST. CLARE OF ASSISI (1194–1253)

Our Father, Hail Mary, Glory Be

Christ Jesus crucified, have mercy on us.

Virgin of all virgins blest!
listen to my fond request:
let me share thy grief divine.

The Fourteenth Station:
Jesus Is Laid in the Tomb

We adore You, O Christ and we praise you.
Because by Your holy cross you have redeemed the world.

"Taking the body, Joseph wrapped it (in) clean linen and laid it in his new tomb that he had hewn in the rock. Then he rolled a huge stone across the entrance to the tomb and departed" (Matthew 27:59–60).

Lord Christ, You have no body on earth but ours, no hands but ours, no feet but ours. Ours are the eyes through which your compassion must look out on the world. Ours are the feet by which you may still go about doing good. Ours are the hands with which you bless people now. Bless our minds and bodies, that we may be a blessing to others.

ST. TERESA OF ÁVILA (1515–1582)

Our Father, Hail Mary, Glory Be

Christ Jesus crucified, have mercy on us.

Christ when Thou shalt call me hence,
be thy Mother my defense,
be Thy Cross my victory.

Closing Prayer

My good and dear Jesus, I kneel before you, asking you most earnestly to engrave upon my heart a deep and lively faith, hope and charity, with true repentance for my sins, and a firm resolve to make amends. As I reflect upon your five wounds, and dwell upon them with a deep compassion and grief, I recall, good Jesus, the words of the Prophet David spoke long ago concerning yourself: "They have pierced my hands and my feet, they have numbered all my bones."

For the intentions of the Holy Father,
   Our Father, Hail Mary, Glory Be

THE LITANY OF THE SAINTS

Lord, have mercy on us.
Lord, have mercy on us.
Christ, have mercy on us.
Christ, have mercy on us.
Lord, have mercy on us.
Lord, have mercy on us.
Christ hear us.
Christ, hear us.
Christ, graciously hear us.

God the Father of heaven,
have mercy on us.
God the Son, Redeemer of the world,
have mercy on us.
God the Holy Spirit,
have mercy on us.
Holy Trinity, One God,
have mercy on us.

Holy Mary,
pray for us. (Say this after each line below.)
Holy Mother of God,
Holy Virgin of virgins,
St. Michael,
St. Gabriel,
St. Raphael,
All you Holy Angels and Archangels,
St. John the Baptist,
St. Joseph,
All you Holy Patriarchs and Prophets,

St. Peter,

St. Paul,

St. Andrew,

St. James,

St. John,

St. Thomas,

St. Philip,

St. Bartholomew,

St. Matthew,

St. Simon,

St. Jude,

St. Matthias,

St. Barnabas,

St. Luke,

St. Mark.

All you holy Apostles and Evangelists,

All you holy Disciples of the Lord,

All you holy Innocents,

St. Stephen,

St. Lawrence,

St. Vincent,

Sts. Fabian and Sebastian,

Sts. John and Paul,

Sts. Cosmos and Damian,

All you holy Martyrs,

St. Sylvester,

St. Gregory,

St. Ambrose,

St. Augustine,

St. Jerome,

St. Martin,

St. Nicholas,

All you holy Bishops and Confessors,

All you holy Doctors,

St. Anthony,

St. Benedict,

St. Bernard,

St. Dominic,

St. Francis,

All you holy Priests and Levites,

All you holy Monks and Hermits,

St. Mary Magdalene,

St. Agatha,

St. Lucy,

St. Agnes,

St. Cecilia,

St. Anastasia,

St. Catherine,

St. Clare,

All you holy Virgins and Widows,

All you holy Saints of God,

Lord be merciful,

Lord, save your people. (Say this after each phrase below.)

from all evil,

from all sin,

from your wrath,

from a sudden and unprovided death,

from the snares of the devil,

from anger, hatred and all ill-will,
from the spirit of uncleanness,
from lightning and tempest,
from the scourge of earthquake,
from plague, famine and war.
from everlasting death,
by the mystery of your holy Incarnation,
by your Coming,
by your Birth,
by your Baptism and holy fasting,
by your Cross and Passion,
by your Death and Burial,
by your holy Resurrection,
by your wonderful Ascension,
by the coming of the Holy Spirit,
on the day of judgment,

Be merciful to us sinners,
   Lord, hear our prayer. (Say this after each phrase below.)
That you will spare us,
That you will pardon us,
That it may please you to bring us to true penance,
Guide and protect your holy Church,
Preserve in holy religion the Pope, and all those in holy Orders,
Humble the enemies of holy Church,
Give peace and unity to the whole Christian people,
Bring back to the unity of the Church all those who are
   straying and bring all unbelievers to the light of the Gospel,
Strengthen and preserve us in your holy service,
Raise our minds to desire the things of heaven,

Reward all our benefactors with eternal blessings,
Deliver our souls from eternal damnation and the souls
of our brethren, relatives, and benefactors,
Give and preserve the fruits of the earth,
Grant eternal rest to all the faithful departed,
That it may please you to hear and heed us,
Jesus, Son of the Living God.

Lamb of God, who takes away the sins of the world,
Spare us, O Lord!
Lamb of God, who takes away the sins of the world,
Graciously hear us, O Lord!
Lamb of God, who takes away the sins of the world,
have mercy on us.

Christ, hear us,
Christ, graciously hear us.
Lord Jesus, hear our prayer,
Lord Jesus, hear our prayer.
Lord, have mercy on us,
Lord, have mercy on us.
Christ, have mercy on us,
Christ, have mercy on us.
Lord, have mercy on us.
Lord, have mercy on us.

CHAPLETS

Rejoice always.
Pray without ceasing.
In all circumstances give thanks.
1 THESSALONIANS 5:16–18

The word chaplet is from the French word meaning "wreath" or "little crown," and is often referred to as a mini-rosary or a small rosary. A chaplet is a set of devotional prayers that honor the Holy Trinity, the Blessed Mother, the angels, or a particular saint. There are many different types of chaplets, yet they are all a series of special prayers intended to deepen your devotion and increase your faith. Chaplets have a different number or arrangement of beads and the number of beads used depends on the prayers. Most chaplets can be recited with ordinary rosary beads. Although chaplets are usually made with beads, they can be made with knots on a string or any method for counting. The Chaplet of Divine Mercy, the Chaplet of St. Michael, the Chaplet of the Seven Sorrows of Mary, and the Chaplet of the Most Precious Blood are among the most recited and beloved chaplets.

THE CHAPLET OF DIVINE MERCY

Your task is to write down everything that I make known to you
about My mercy, for the benefit of those who by reading
these things will be comforted in their souls and
will have the courage to approach me.

DIVINE MERCY IN MY SOUL (1693)*

St. Maria Faustina Kowalska (1905–1938) was a Polish nun, visionary, and the apostle of Divine Mercy. She was a member of the Congregation of Sisters of Our Lady of Mercy in Poland. Beginning in 1931, and until her death in 1938, she received visitations and revelations from Jesus. In 1934, as instructed by our Lord, she began recording these mystical experiences in a personal diary, *Divine Mercy in My Soul*. St. Faustina was canonized by Blessed Pope John Paul II on April 30, 2000, the first Sunday after Easter, on Divine Mercy Sunday. The Catholic Church celebrates the feast of St. Faustina on October 5.

How to Pray the Chaplet

In his revelations to St. Faustina, Jesus entrusted to her the Chaplet of Divine Mercy. Jesus said to her, as stated in *Divine Mercy in My Soul:* "Say unceasingly the chaplet that I have taught you. Whoever will recite it will receive great mercy at the hour of death. Priests will recommend it to sinners as their last hope of salvation. Even if there were a sinner most hardened, if he were to recite this chaplet only once, he would receive grace from My infinite mercy. I desire that the whole world know My infinite mercy. I desire to grant unimaginable graces to those souls who trust in My Mercy (687).

*The numerals in parentheses in this chapter correspond with the paragraph numbers found in the margins of St. Faustina's diary, *Divine Mercy in My Soul*.

"At the hour of their death, I defend as My own glory every soul that will say this chaplet; or when others say it for a dying person, the pardon is the same. When this chaplet is said by the bedside of a dying person, God's anger is placated, unfathomable mercy envelops the soul, and the very depths of My tender mercy are moved for the sake of the sorrowful Passion of My Son (811)."

The Lord made it clear to St. Faustina that the chaplet was not just for her but for the whole world. Jesus attached extraordinary promises to all those who recite the chaplet: "Encourage souls to say the chaplet which I have given to you. It pleases Me to grant everything they ask of Me by saying the chaplet. When hardened sinners say it, I will fill their souls with peace, and the hour of their death will be a happy one....When they say this chaplet in the presence of the dying, I will stand between My Father and the dying person, not as the just Judge but as the merciful Savior (1541).

"The souls that say this chaplet will be embraced by My mercy during their lifetime and especially at the hour of their death. (754)

"Oh, what great graces I will grant to souls who say this chaplet: the very depths of My tender mercy are stirred for the sake of those who say the chaplet (848)."

The Lord said to St. Faustina: "This prayer will serve to appease My wrath. You will recite it for nine days, on the beads of the rosary, in the following manner: First of all, you will say one OUR FATHER and HAIL MARY and the I BELIEVE IN GOD. Then on the OUR FATHER beads you will say the following words: Eternal Father, I offer You the Body and Blood, Soul and Divinity of Your dearly beloved Son, Our Lord Jesus Christ, in atonement for our sins and those of the whole world. On the HAIL MARY beads you will say the following words: For the sake of His sorrowful Passion, have mercy on us and on the whole world. In conclusion, three times you will recite these words: Holy God, Holy Mighty One, Holy Immortal One, Have mercy on us and on the whole world (476)."

I have provided passages from Scripture to contemplate as you pray the Chaplet of Divine Mercy. Each Scripture verse, along with the powerful words, "For the sake of His sorrowful passion, have mercy on us and on the whole world," will touch your heart and help you realize just what our Lord went through in his passion for each one of us and prayerfully pleads the mercy of God upon us.

THE CHAPLET OF DIVINE MERCY

Our Father

Our Father, who art in heaven,
hallowed be thy name;
thy kingdom come;
thy will be done, on earth as it is in heaven.
Give us this day our daily bread;
and forgive us our trespasses
as we forgive those who trespass
against us;
and lead us not into temptation,
but deliver us from evil. Amen.

Hail Mary

Hail Mary, full of grace, the Lord is with you;
blessed are you among women,
and blessed is the fruit of Thy womb, Jesus.

Holy Mary, Mother of God,
pray for us sinners
now and at the hour of our death. Amen.

Apostles' Creed

I believe in God,
the Father almighty,
Creator of heaven and earth,
and in Jesus Christ, his only Son, our Lord,
who was conceived by the Holy Spirit,
born of the Virgin Mary,
suffered under Pontius Pilate,
was crucified, died, and was buried;
he descended into hell;
on the third day he rose again from the dead;
he ascended into heaven,
and is seated at the right hand of God, the Father Almighty;
from there he will come to judge the living and the dead.

I believe in the Holy Spirit,
the holy catholic Church,
the communion of saints,
the forgiveness of sins,
the resurrection of the body,
and life everlasting. Amen.

Eternal Father, I offer you the Body and Blood, Soul and Divinity of your dearly beloved Son, Our Lord Jesus Christ, in atonement for your sins and those of the world.

"Then Jesus came with them to a place called Gethsemane" (Matthew 26:36).

For the sake of His sorrowful Passion,
have mercy on us and on the whole world.
(Say this prayer after each Scripture passage below.)

"He said to his disciples, 'Sit here while I go over there and pray'" (Matthew 26:36).

"He took along Peter and the two sons of Zebedee, and began to feel sorrow and distress" (Matthew 26:37).

"Then he said to them, 'My soul is sorrowful even to death. Remain here and keep watch with me'" (Matthew 26:38).

"He advanced a little and fell prostrate in prayer, saying..." (Matthew 26:39).

"'My Father, if it is possible, let this cup pass from me; yet, not as I will, but as you will'" (Matthew 26:39).

"When he returned to his disciples he found them asleep" (Matthew 26:40).

"He said to Peter, 'So you could not keep watch with me for one hour?'" (Matthew 26:40)

"Watch and pray that you may not undergo the test. The spirit is willing, but the flesh is weak" (Matthew 26:41).

"'The hour is at hand when the Son of Man is to be handed over to sinners....Look, my betrayer is at hand'" (Matthew 26:45–46).

Eternal Father, I offer you the Body and Blood, Soul and Divinity of your dearly beloved Son, Our Lord Jesus Christ, in atonement for your sins and those of the world.

"They bound Jesus, led him away, and handed him over to Pilate" (Mark 15:1).

For the sake of His sorrowful Passion,
have mercy on us and on the whole world.
(Say this prayer after each Scripture passage below.)

"Pilate questioned him, 'Are you the king of the Jews?'" (Mark 15:2).

"Jesus answered, 'My kingdom does not belong to this world'" (John 18:36).

"Then Pilate took Jesus and had him scourged" (John 19:1).

"He was spurned and avoided by men, a man of suffering" (Isaiah 53:3).

"Yet it was our pain that he bore, our sufferings he endured" (Isaiah 53:4).

"But he was pierced for our sins, crushed for our iniquity" (Isaiah 53:5).

"He bore the punishment that makes us whole, by his wounds we were healed" (Isaiah 53:5).

"The men who held Jesus in custody were ridiculing and beating him" (Luke 22:63).

"They blindfolded him and questioned him, saying, 'Prophesy! "Who is it that struck you?"'" (Luke 22:64).

Eternal Father, I offer you the Body and Blood, Soul and Divinity of your dearly beloved Son, Our Lord Jesus Christ, in atonement for your sins and those of the world.

"Then the soldiers of the governor took Jesus inside the praetorium and gathered the whole cohort around him" (Matthew 27:27).

For the sake of His sorrowful Passion,
have mercy on us and on the whole world.
(Say this prayer after each Scripture passage below.)

"They stripped off his clothes and threw a scarlet military cloak about him" (Matthew 27:28).

"Then weaving a crown out of thorns, they placed it on his head, and a reed in his right hand" (Matthew 27:29).

"And kneeling before him, they mocked him, saying, 'Hail, King of the Jews!'" (Matthew 27:29).

"They spat upon him" (Matthew 27:30).

"And took the reed and kept striking him on the head" (Matthew 27:30).

"So Jesus came out, wearing the crown of thorns and the purple cloak" (John 19:5).

"And he said to them, 'Behold, your king!' But they continued their shouting,, 'Crucify him! Crucify him!'" (Luke 23:21).

"And when they had mocked him, they stripped him of the cloak, dressed him in his own clothes" (Matthew 27:31).

"Then he handed him over to them to be crucified" (John 19:16).

Eternal Father, I offer you the Body and Blood, Soul and Divinity of your dearly beloved Son, Our Lord Jesus Christ, in atonement for your sins and those of the world.

"And carrying the cross himself, they led him out to crucify him" (John 19:17, Mark 15:20).

For the sake of His sorrowful Passion,
have mercy on us and on the whole world.
(Say this prayer after each Scripture passage below.)

"Though harshly treated, he submitted and did not open his mouth" (Isaiah 53:7).

"Like a lamb led to slaughter...he did not open his mouth" (Isaiah 53:7).

"As they led him away, they took hold of a certain Simon, a Cyrenian...and made him carry the cross behind Jesus" (Luke 23:26).

"A large crowd of people followed Jesus, including many women who mourned and lamented him" (Luke 23:27).

"Jesus turned to them and said, 'Daughters of Jerusalem, do not weep for me; weep instead for yourselves and for your children'" (Luke 23:28).

"'If anyone wishes to come after me, he must deny himself'" (Luke 9:23).

"'And take up his cross daily and follow me'" (Luke 9:23).

"They brought Jesus to the place of Golgotha, which is translated Place of the Skull" (Mark 15:22).

"There they crucified him, and with him two others" (John 19:18).

Eternal Father, I offer you the Body and Blood, Soul and Divinity of your dearly beloved Son, Our Lord Jesus Christ, in atonement for your sins and those of the world.

"(Then Jesus said, 'Father, forgive them; they know not what they do')" (Luke 23:34).

For the sake of His sorrowful Passion,
have mercy on us and on the whole world.
(Say this prayer after each line of Scripture below.)

"Then he said, 'Jesus, remember me when you come into your kingdom'" (Luke 23:42).

"And he replied to him, 'Amen, I say to you, today you will be with me in Paradise'" (Luke 23:43).

"When Jesus saw his mother and the disciple there whom he loved, he said to his mother, 'Woman, behold, your son'" (John 19:26).

"Then he said to the disciple, 'Behold, your mother'" (John 19:27).

"And about three o'clock Jesus cried out in a loud voice...'My God, my God, why have you forsaken me?'" (Matthew 27:46).

"Aware that everything was now finished, in order that the scripture might be fulfilled, Jesus said, 'I thirst'" (John 19:28).

"When Jesus had taken the wine, he said, 'It is finished'" (John 19:30).

"Jesus cried out in a loud voice, 'Father, into your hands I commend my spirit'" (Luke 23:46).

"And bowing his head, he gave up his spirit" (John 19:30, from the *Jerusalem Bible*).

Concluding Prayer (repeat three times)

Holy God, Holy Mighty One, Holy Immortal One,
have mercy on us and on the whole world.

Prayers Written by St. Faustina

Eternal God, in whom mercy is endless and the treasury of compassion inexhaustible, look kindly upon us and increase Your mercy in us, that in difficult moments we might not despair nor become despondent, but with great confidence submit ourselves to Your holy will, which is Love and Mercy itself (950).

****

Everything begins with Your mercy
and ends with Your mercy (1506).

****

I fly to Your mercy, Compassionate God, who alone are good. Although my misery is great, and my offenses are many, I trust in Your mercy, because You are the God of mercy; and, from time immemorial, it has never been heard of, nor do heaven or earth remember, that a soul trusting in Your mercy has been disappointed (1730).

O incomprehensible and limitless Mercy Divine, to extol and adore You worthily, who can? Supreme attribute of Almighty God, You are the sweet hope for sinful man. Into one hymn yourselves unite, stars, earth and sea, and in one accord, thankfully and fervently sing of the incomprehensible Divine Mercy (951).

****

God is Love, Goodness and Mercy (1148).

****

O Greatly Merciful God, Infinite Goodness, today all mankind calls out from the abyss of its misery to Your mercy—to Your compassion, O God; and it is with its mighty voice of misery that it cries out.

Gracious God, do not reject the prayer of this earth's exiles! O Lord, Goodness beyond our understanding, Who are acquainted with our misery through and through, and know that by our own power we cannot ascend to You, we implore You: anticipate us with Your grace and keep on increasing Your mercy in us, that we may faithfully do Your holy will all through our life and at death's hour.

Let the omnipotence of Your mercy shield us from the darts of our salvation's enemies, that we may with confidence, as Your children, await Your final coming—that day known to You alone. And we expect to obtain everything promised us by Jesus in spite of all our wretchedness. For Jesus is our Hope: Through His merciful Heart, as through an open gate, we pass through to heaven (1570).

****

*The Mother of God...has taught me
how to love God interiorly (40).*

****

O Mary, my Mother and my Lady, I offer You my soul, my body, my life and my death, and all that will follow it. I place everything in Your hands. O my Mother, cover my soul with Your virginal mantle and grant me the grace of purity of heart, soul and body. Defend me with Your power against all enemies, and especially against those who hide their malice behind the mask of virtue. O lovely lily! You are for me a mirror, O my Mother! (79)

Fortify my soul that pain will not break it. Mother of grace, teach me to live by (the power) of God. (315)

O Mary, my sweet Mother,…be the safeguard of my life, especially at death's hour, in the final fight (161).

****

*St. Joseph urged me to have a
constant devotion to him (1203).*

****

Memorare

Remember, O most pure spouse of Mary, and my dearly beloved guardian, St. Joseph, that never was it known that anyone who invoked your care and requested your help was left without consolation. Inspired with this confidence, I come to you, and with all the ardor of my spirit I commend myself to you. Do not reject my prayer, O Foster Father of the Savior, but graciously receive and answer it. Amen.

~ *St. Faustina wrote in her diary: "St. Joseph himself told me to recite three prayers (the Our Father, Hail Mary, and Glory Be) and the Memorare once every day" (1203).*

Short Aspirations

Do what You will with me, O Jesus; I will adore You in everything. May Your will be done in me, O my Lord and my God, and I will praise Your infinite mercy (78).

O my God, my only hope, I have placed all my trust in You, and I know I shall not be disappointed (317).

Jesus, I trust in You (1209).

My Jesus, make my heart like unto Your merciful Heart. Jesus, help me to go through life doing good to everyone (692).

Jesus, Life and Truth, my Master, guide every step of my life, that I may act according to Your holy will (688).

O Savior of the world. I unite myself with Your mercy. My Jesus, I join all my sufferings to Yours and deposit them in the treasury of the Church for the benefit of souls (740).

****

In all things, I depend on God
with unwavering trust (1400).

****

St. Faustina, you told us that your mission would continue after your death and that you would not forget us (1582).

Our Lord also granted you a great privilege, telling you to "distribute graces as you will, to whom you will, and when you will" (31).

Relying on this, I ask your intercession for the graces I need, especially to be faithful to the inspirations of the Holy Spirit and to be a saint.

Help me, above all, to trust in Jesus as you did and thus to glorify His mercy and goodness every moment of my life.

Prayer to Obtain Graces
Through the Intercession of St. Faustina

O Jesus, who filled St. Faustina with profound veneration for your boundless Mercy, deign, if it be Your holy will, to grant me, through her intercession, the grace for which I fervently pray—My sins render me unworthy of Your Mercy, but be mindful of St. Faustina's spirit of sacrifice and self-denial, and reward her virtue by granting the petition which, with childlike trust, I present to You through her intercession.

Our Father, Hail Mary, Glory Be.

~ St. Faustina, pray for us.

****

God's love is the flower ~ Mercy is the fruit.
Let the doubting soul read these considerations
on Divine Mercy and become trusting (948).

****

The Litany to the Divine Mercy

Divine Mercy, gushing forth from the bosom of the Father,
I trust in You.
Divine Mercy, greatest attribute of God,
I trust in You.
Divine Mercy, incomprehensible mystery,
I trust in You.
Divine Mercy, fount gushing forth from the mystery of the Most
Blessed Trinity,
I trust in You.
Divine Mercy, unfathomed by any intellect, human or angelic,
I trust in You.
Divine Mercy, from which wells forth all life and happiness,
I trust in You.
Divine Mercy, better than the heavens,
I trust in You.
Divine Mercy, source of miracles and wonders,
I trust in You.
Divine Mercy, encompassing the whole universe,
I trust in You.

Divine Mercy, descending to earth in the Person of the Incarnate
Word,
I trust in You.
Divine Mercy, which flowed out from the open wound of the Heart
of Jesus,
I trust in You.
Divine Mercy, enclosed in the Heart of Jesus for us, and especially
for sinners,
I trust in You.

Divine Mercy, unfathomed in the institution of the Sacred Host,
I trust in You.
Divine Mercy, in the founding of Holy Church,
I trust in You.
Divine Mercy, in the Sacrament of Holy Baptism,
I trust in You.
Divine Mercy, in our justification through Jesus Christ,
I trust in You.
Divine Mercy, accompanying us through our whole life,
I trust in You.
Divine Mercy, embracing us especially at the hour of death,
I trust in You.
Divine Mercy, endowing us with immortal life,
I trust in You.
Divine Mercy, accompanying us every moment of our life,
I trust in You.
Divine Mercy, shielding us from the fire of hell,
I trust in You.
Divine Mercy, in the conversion of hardened sinners,
I trust in You.
Divine Mercy, astonishment for Angels, incomprehensible to Saints,
I trust in You.
Divine Mercy, unfathomed in all the mysteries of God,
I trust in You.
Divine Mercy, lifting us out of every misery,
I trust in You.
Divine Mercy, source of our happiness and joy,
I trust in You.
Divine Mercy, in calling us forth from nothingness to existence,
I trust in You.

Divine Mercy, embracing all the works of His hands,
I trust in You.

Divine Mercy, crown of all of God's handiwork,
I trust in You.

Divine Mercy, in which we are all immersed,
I trust in You.

Divine Mercy, sweet relief for anguished hearts,
I trust in You.

Divine Mercy, only hope of despairing souls,
I trust in You.

Divine Mercy, repose of hearts, peace amidst fear,
I trust in You.

Divine Mercy, delight and ecstasy of holy souls,
I trust in You.

Divine Mercy, inspiring hope against all hope,
I trust in You. (949).

****

*Let the glory and praise to The Divine Mercy
rise from every creature throughout all ages and times (1005).*

****

THE CHAPLET OF ST. MICHAEL

*Make the holy Angels your friends. Give them joy by having
confidential recourse to them and honor them by your prayers,
for they are ever near, to comfort and protect you.*
ST. BERNARD

The Chaplet of St. Michael is a devotion honoring St. Michael the
Archangel and all nine Choirs of Angels. The chaplet consists of

nine salutations, one to each of the nine Choirs of Angels. Begin the chaplet with the opening invocation and one Glory Be. Pray one Our Father and three Hail Marys after each of the nine salutations. The chaplet concludes with four Our Fathers honoring the Archangels Michael, Gabriel, Raphael, and your Guardian Angel and then finishes with a closing prayer.

O God, come to my assistance,
O Lord, make haste to help me.

Glory be to the Father, the Son, and the Holy Spirit;
as it was in the beginning, is now, and ever shall be,
world without end. Amen.

THE FIRST SALUTATION

One Our Father, three Hail Marys to the First Angelic Choir

At the intercession of St. Michael and the heavenly choir of the Seraphim, may it please God to make us worthy to receive into our hearts the fire of his perfect charity. Amen.

THE SECOND SALUTATION

One Our Father, three Hail Marys to the Second Angelic Choir

At the intercession of St. Michael and the heavenly choir of the Cherubim, may God grant us grace to abandon the ways of sin, and follow the path of Christian perfection. Amen.

THE THIRD SALUTATION

One Our Father, three Hail Marys to the Third Angelic Choir

At the intercession of St. Michael and the sacred choir of the Thrones, may it please God to infuse into our hearts a true and earnest spirit of humility. Amen.

THE FOURTH SALUTATION

One Our Father, three Hail Marys to the Fourth Angelic Choir

At the intercession of St. Michael and the heavenly choir of the Dominations, may it please God to grant us grace to have dominion over our senses, and to correct our depraved passions. Amen.

THE FIFTH SALUTATION

One Our Father, three Hail Marys to the Fifth Angelic Choir

At the intercession of St. Michael and the heavenly choir of the Powers, may God vouchsafe to keep our souls from the wiles and temptations of the devil. Amen.

THE SIXTH SALUTATION

One Our Father, three Hail Marys to the Sixth Angelic Choir

At the intercession of St. Michael and the choir of the admirable celestial Virtues, may our Lord keep us from falling into temptations and deliver us from evil. Amen.

THE SEVENTH SALUTATION

One Our Father, three Hail Marys to the Seventh Angelic Choir

At the intercession of St. Michael and the heavenly choir of the Principalities, may it please God to fill our souls with the spirit of true and hearty obedience. Amen.

THE EIGHTH SALUTATION

One Our Father, three Hail Marys to the Eighth Angelic Choir

At the intercession of St. Michael and the heavenly choir of Archangels, may it please God to grant us the gift of perseverance in the faith and in all good works, that we may thereby be enabled to attain unto the glory of Paradise. Amen.

THE NINTH SALUTATION

One Our Father, three Hail Marys to the Ninth Angelic Choir

At the intercession of St. Michael and the heavenly choir of Angels, may God vouchsafe to grant that the Holy Angels may protect us during life, and after death may lead us into the everlasting glory of heaven. Amen.

~ Then pray the Our Father four times in conclusion, the first in honor of St. Michael, the second in honor of St. Gabriel, the third in honor of St. Raphael, and the fourth in honor of our Guardian Angel. Then end with the following antiphon:

St. Michael, glorious Prince, chief and champion of the heavenly hosts, guardian of the souls of men, conqueror of the rebellious angels, steward of the Palace of God under our Divine King Jesus Christ; our worthy leader, endowed with superhuman excellence and virtue; vouchsafe to free us from all evil, who with full confidence have recourse to thee; and by thy powerful protection, enable us to make progress every day in the faithful service to our God. Amen.

Pray for us, most blessed St. Michael, Prince of the Church of Jesus Christ. That we may be made worthy of his promises.

Let us pray: Almighty and Eternal God, who in Thy Own marvelous goodness and pity, didst, for the common salvation of men, choose the glorious Archangel Michael, to be the Prince of thy Church; make us worthy, we pray Thee, to be delivered by his beneficent protection from all our enemies, that, at the hour of our death none of them may approach to harm us; and that by the same Archangel Michael we may be introduced into the Presence of Thy Most High and Heavenly Majesty. Through the Merits of Jesus Christ our Lord. Amen.

PRAYERS TO THE HOLY ANGELS

Prayer to St. Michael the Archangel

St. Michael the Archangel, defend us in battle. Be our defense against the wickedness and snares of the Devil. May God rebuke him, we humbly pray, and do thou, O Prince of heavenly hosts, by the power of God, thrust into hell Satan, and all evil spirits, who prowl about the world seeking the ruin of souls. Amen.

~ St. Padre Pio had a great devotion to his guardian angel: Invoke often this Guardian Angel, this benevolent Angel and repeat often this beautiful prayer...

Prayer to Your Guardian Angel

Angel of God, my guardian dear, to whom God's love commits me here, ever this day, (or night) be at my side to light and guard, to rule and guide. Amen.

~ Pray one Our Father to honor the guardian angel of your spouse, children or loved ones.

****

The Angels take great pleasure in helping us with our enterprises, when they are in accordance with God's will.
ST. JOHN VIANNEY

****

Prayer to St. Gabriel the Archangel

Glorious Archangel Gabriel, God chose you to deliver His message and be part of that great moment in the history of mankind's redemption, as the word was made flesh at your announcement. Sacred

Scripture reveals to us that your last words to our Blessed Mother at that momentous occasion were "nothing is impossible with God." Truly believing in this, O mighty Prince to the heavenly court, I turn to you in this time of need. Kindly assist me to embrace more fervently to my heart the Redeemer of the world. Present my earnest petition to God to obtain for me (request) if it be His will. Amen.

Blessed be God in His Angels and in His Saints.

Prayer to St. Raphael the Archangel

Glorious Archangel St. Raphael, great prince of the heavenly court, you are illustrious for your gifts of wisdom and grace. You are a guide of those who journey by land or sea or air, consoler of the afflicted, and refuge of sinners. I beg you, assist me in all my needs and in all the sufferings of this life, as once you helped the young Tobias on his travels. Because you are the "medicine of God" I humbly pray you to heal the many infirmities of my soul and the ills that afflict my body. I especially ask of you the favor (request), and the great grace of purity to prepare me to be the temple of the Holy Spirit. Amen.

~ The Catholic Church celebrates the feast of
Sts. Michael, Gabriel, and Raphael on September 29,
and the Holy Guardian Angels on October 2.

All you holy Angels and Archangels,
Thrones and Dominations,
Principalities and Powers,
the Virtues of heaven,
Cherubim and Seraphim,
Praise the Lord Forever. Amen.

The Litany of the Holy Angels

Lord, have mercy.
Lord, have mercy.
Christ, have mercy.
Christ, have mercy.
Lord, have mercy.
Lord, have mercy.
Christ, hear us.
Christ, graciously hear us.

God the Father of Heaven,
have mercy on us.
God the Son, Redeemer of the world,
have mercy on us.
God the Holy Ghost,
have mercy on us.
Holy Trinity, One God,
have mercy on us.

Holy Mary, Queen of Angels,
pray for us.
Holy Mother of God,
pray for us.
Holy Virgin of virgins,
pray for us.

St. Michael, who wast ever the defender of the people of God,
pray for us. (Say this after each phrase below.)
St. Michael, who didst drive from Heaven lucifer and his rebel crew,
St. Michael, who didst cast down to Hell the accuser of our brethren,

St. Gabriel, who didst expound to Daniel the heavenly vision,
St. Gabriel, who didst foretell to Zachary the birth and ministry
   of John the Baptist,
St. Gabriel, who didst announce to Blessed Mary the incarnation
   of the Divine Word,

St. Raphael, who didst lead Tobias safely through his journey to
   his home again,
St. Raphael, who didst deliver Sara from the devil,
St. Raphael, who didst restore his sight to Tobias the elder,

All ye holy Angels, who stand around the high and lofty Throne
   Of God,
Who cry to Him continually: Holy, Holy, Holy,
Who dispel the darkness of our minds and give us light,
Who are the messengers of heavenly things to men,
Who have been appointed by God to be our guardians,
Who always behold the Face of our Father Who is in Heaven,
Who rejoice over one sinner doing penance,
Who struck the Sodomites with blindness,
Who led Lot out of the midst of the ungodly,
Who ascended and descended on the ladder of Jacob,
Who delivered the Divine Law to Moses on Mount Sinai,
Who brought good tidings when Christ was born,
Who ministered to Him in the desert,
Who comforted Him in His agony,
Who sat in white garments at His sepulcher,
Who appeared to the disciples as He went up into Heaven,
Who shall go before Him bearing the standard of the Cross when
   He comes to judgment,

Who shall gather together the elect at the End of the World,
Who shall separate the wicked from among the just,
Who offer to God the prayers of those who pray,
Who assist us at the hour of death,

Who carried Lazarus into Abraham's bosom,
Who conduct to Heaven the souls of the just,
Who perform signs and wonders by the power of God,
Who are sent to minister for those who shall receive the inheritance
       of salvation,
Who are set over kingdoms and provinces,
Who have often put to flight armies of enemies,
Who have often delivered God's servants from prison and other
       perils of this life,
Who have often consoled the holy martyrs in their torments,
Who are wont to cherish with peculiar care the prelates and princes
       of the Church,
All ye holy orders of blessed spirits,

From all dangers,
    deliver us, O Lord. (Say this after each phrase below.)
From the snares of the devil,
From all heresy and schism,
From plague, famine, and war,
From sudden and unlooked-for death,
From everlasting death,

We sinners,
    Beseech Thee to hear us.

Through Thy holy Angels,
we beseech Thee, hear us. (Say this after each phrase below.)
That Thou wouldst spare us,
That Thou wouldst pardon us,
That Thou wouldst govern and preserve Thy Holy Church,
That Thou wouldst protect our Apostolic Prelate and
        all ecclesiastical orders,
That Thou wouldst grant peace and security to kings and
        all Christian princes,
That Thou wouldst give and preserve the fruits of the earth,
That Thou wouldst grant eternal rest to all the faithful departed,

Lamb of God, Who takest away the sins of the world,
spare us, O Lord.
Lamb of God, Who takest away the sins of the world,
Graciously hear us, O Lord.
Lamb of God, Who takest away the sins of the world,
have mercy on us.

Lord, have mercy.
Christ, have mercy.
Lord, have mercy.

Our Father, Hail Mary, Glory Be

Bless the Lord, all ye Angels:
Ye who are mighty in strength, who fulfill His commandments,
hearkening unto the voice of His words.
He hath given His Angels charge concerning thee,
To keep thee in all thy ways.

Let us pray.

O God, Who dost arrange the services of Angels and men in a wonderful order, mercifully grant that our life may be protected on earth by those who always do Thee service in Heaven, through Jesus Christ Thy Son, Who with Thee and the Holy Ghost art one God now and forever. Amen.

O God, Who in Thine unspeakable Providence dost send Thine Angels to keep guard over us, grant unto Thy suppliants that we may be continually defended by their protection and may rejoice eternally in their society, through Jesus Christ our Lord, Who liveth and reigneth with Thee, in the unity of the Holy Ghost, forever and ever. Amen.

THE CHAPLET OF THE
SEVEN SORROWS OF MARY

O lady, by the love which
you bear Jesus, help me to love Him.
ST. BRIDGET OF SWEDEN

The Chaplet of the Seven Sorrows of Mary consists of forty-nine Hail Marys divided into groups of seven. Each group of seven Hail Marys represents an event in Mary's life in which sorrow most pierced her heart. The chaplet begins after the optional opening prayer and the Act of Contrition. Announce the first sorrow and pray one Our Father. Then pray seven Hail Marys. I have provided Scripture verses for each Hail Mary that can be reflected upon before reciting each Hail Mary. Praying with Scripture is truly a powerful way to pray as it provides inspiration before every Hail Mary bringing the sorrows Mary endured to life for us. We reflect with love (and sorrow) on those moments in our Blessed Mother's life which brought her the most suffering. Continue the chaplet in the same manner for the remaining six sorrows. The Chaplet of the Seven Sorrows of Mary concludes with three Hail Marys in honor of the tears of our Sorrowful Mother.

Opening Prayer to Our Lady of Sorrows

Mary, most holy Virgin and Queen of Martyrs, accept the sincere homage of my filial affection. Into thy heart, pierced by so many swords, do thou welcome my poor soul. Receive it as the companion of thy sorrows at the foot of the Cross, on which Jesus died for the redemption of the world. With thee, O sorrowful Virgin, I will gladly suffer all the trials, contradictions, and infirmities which it shall please our Lord to send me. I offer them all to thee in memory of thy sorrows, so that every thought of my mind, and every beat of my heart may be an act of compassion and of love for thee. And do thou, sweet Mother, have pity on me, reconcile me to thy divine Son Jesus, keep me in His grace and assist me in my last agony, so that I may be able to meet thee in Heaven and sing thy glories. Amen (the *Raccolta*, No. 384).

Act of Contrition

O my God, I am heartily sorry for having offended Thee, and I detest all my sins because I dread the loss of Heaven and the pains of Hell, but most of all because they offend Thee, my God, Who art all good and deserving of all my love. I firmly resolve with the help of Thy grace to confess my sins, to do penance, and to amend my life. Amen.

THE PRAYERS OF THE
CHAPLET OF THE SEVEN SORROWS

The First Sorrow of Mary:
The Prophecy of Simeon

Our Father

"When the days were completed for their purification according to the law of Moses, they took him up to Jerusalem to present him to the Lord" (Luke 2:22).

Hail Mary

"Now there was a man in Jerusalem whose name was Simeon. This man was righteous and devout...and the holy Spirit was upon him" (Luke 2:25).

Hail Mary

"He came in the Spirit into the temple; and when the parents brought in the child Jesus to perform the custom of the law in regard to him..." (Luke 2:27).

Hail Mary

"He took him into his arms and blessed God saying: 'Now, Master, you may let your servant go in peace, according to your word, for my eyes have seen your salvation, which you prepared in sight of all the peoples, a light for revelation to the Gentiles, and glory for your people Israel'" (Luke 2:28–32).

Hail Mary

"The child's father and mother were amazed at what was said about him; and Simeon blessed them and said to Mary his mother..." (Luke 2:33–34).

Hail Mary

"'Behold, this child is destined for the fall and rise of many in Israel, and to be a sign that will be contradicted'" (Luke 2:34).

Hail Mary

"(and you yourself a sword will pierce) so that the thoughts of many hearts may be revealed" (Luke 2:35).

Hail Mary

Mary, Our Mother of Sorrows, pray for us.

The Second Sorrow of Mary: The Flight Into Egypt

Our Father

"When they had departed, behold, the angel of the Lord appeared to Joseph in a dream and said..." (Matthew 2:13).

Hail Mary

"Rise, take the child and his mother, flee to Egypt, and stay there until I tell you. Herod is going to search for the child to destroy him" (Matthew 2:13).

Hail Mary

"Joseph rose and took the child and his mother by night and departed for Egypt" (Matthew 2:14).

Hail Mary

"When Herod realized that he had been deceived by the magi, he became furious" (Matthew 2:16).

Hail Mary

"He ordered the massacre of all the boys in Bethlehem and its vicinity two years old and under, in accordance with the time he had ascertained from the magi" (Matthew 2:16).

Hail Mary

"Then was fulfilled what had been said through Jeremiah the prophet: 'A voice was heard in Ramah, sobbing and loud lamentation...'" (Matthew 2:17–18).

Hail Mary

"Rachel weeping for her children, and she would not be consoled, since they were no more'" (Matthew 2:18).

Hail Mary

Mary, Our Mother of Sorrows, pray for us.

The Third Sorrow of Mary:
The Loss of Jesus in the Temple

Our Father

"Each year his parents went to Jerusalem for the feast of Passover, and when he was twelve years old, they went up according to festival custom" (Luke 2:41–42).

Hail Mary

"After they had completed its days, as they were returning, the boy Jesus remained behind in Jerusalem..." (Luke 2:43).

Hail Mary

"But his parents did not know it. Thinking that he was in the caravan, they journeyed for a day..." (Luke 2:43–44).

Hail Mary

"And looked for him among their relatives and acquaintances, but not finding him, they returned to Jerusalem to look for him" (Luke 2:44–45).

Hail Mary

"After three days they found him in the temple, sitting in the midst of the teachers, listening to them and asking them questions" (Luke 2:46).

Hail Mary

"His mother said to him, 'Son, why have you done this to us? Your father and I have been looking for you with great anxiety'" (Luke 2:48).

Hail Mary

"He said to them, 'Why were you looking for me? Did you not know that I must be in my Father's house?'" (Luke 2:49).

Hail Mary

Mary, Our Mother of Sorrows, pray for us.

The Fourth Sorrow of Mary:
Mary Meets Jesus on the Way to Calvary

Our Father

"And carrying the cross himself he went out..." (John 19:17).

Hail Mary

"They took hold of a certain Simon, a Cyrenian...and...made him carry [the cross] behind Jesus" (Luke 23:26).

Hail Mary

"A large crowd of people followed Jesus, including many women who mourned and lamented him" (Luke 23:27).

Hail Mary

"Jesus turned to them and said, 'Daughters of Jerusalem, do not weep for me; weep instead for yourselves and for your children'" (Luke 23:28).

Hail Mary

"They brought him to the place of Golgotha (which is translated Place of the Skull)" (Mark 15:22).

Hail Mary

"They gave him wine drugged with myrrh, but he did not take it" (Mark 15:23).

Hail Mary

"Then they crucified him, and divided his garments by casting lots for them" (Mark 15:24).

Hail Mary

Mary, Our Mother of Sorrows, pray for us.

The Fifth Sorrow of Mary:
Jesus Dies on the Cross

Our Father

"(Then Jesus said, 'Father, forgive them, they know not what they do')" (Luke 23:34).

Hail Mary

"When Jesus saw his mother and the disciple there whom he loved, he said to his mother, 'Woman, behold, your son'" (John 19:26).

Hail Mary

"Then he said to the disciple, 'Behold, your mother'" (John 19:27).

Hail Mary

"About three o'clock, Jesus cried out in a loud voice, *'Eli, Eli, lema sabachthani?'* Which means, 'My God, my God, why have you forsaken me?'" (Matthew 27:46).

Hail Mary

"Aware that everything was now finished, in order that the scriptures might be fulfilled, Jesus said, 'I thirst'" (John 19:28).

Hail Mary

"When Jesus had taken the wine, he said, 'It is finished'" (John 19:30).

Hail Mary

"Jesus cried out in a loud voice, 'Father, into your hands I commend my spirit'; and when he had said this he breathed his last" (Luke 23:46).

Hail Mary

> *Mary, Our Mother of Sorrows, pray for us.*

The Sixth Sorrow of Mary:
Jesus Is Taken Down From the Cross

Our Father

"Now since it was preparation day, in order that the bodies might not remain on the cross on the sabbath...the Jews asked Pilate that their legs be broken and they be taken down" (John 19:31).

Hail Mary

"So the soldiers came and broke the legs of the first and then of the other one who was crucified with Jesus" (John 19:32).

Hail Mary

"But when they came to Jesus and saw that he was already dead, they did not break his legs..." (John 19:33).

Hail Mary

"But one soldier thrust his lance into his side, and immediately blood and water flowed out" (John 19:34).

Hail Mary

"Joseph of Arimathea, a distinguished member of the council… came and courageously went to Pilate, and asked for the body of Jesus" (Mark 15:43).

Hail Mary

"Pilate was amazed that he was already dead....He gave the body to Joseph" (Mark 15:44–45).

Hail Mary

"Having bought a linen cloth, he took him down, wrapped him in the linen cloth" (Mark 15:46).

Hail Mary

   Mary, Our Mother of Sorrows, pray for us.

The Seventh Sorrow of Mary:
Jesus Is Laid in the Tomb

Our Father

"Nicodemus…also came bringing a mixture of myrrh and aloes weighing about one hundred pounds" (John 19:39).

Hail Mary

"They took the body of Jesus and bound it with burial cloths along with the spices, according to the Jewish burial custom" (John 19:40).

Hail Mary

"Now in the place where he had been crucified there was a garden..." (John 19:41).

Hail Mary

"And in the garden a new tomb, in which no one had yet been buried" (John 19:41).

Hail Mary

"A tomb...had been hewn out of the rock" (Mark 15:46).

Hail Mary

"So they laid Jesus there because of the Jewish preparation day; for the tomb was close by" (John 19:42).

Hail Mary

"Then [Joseph] rolled a huge stone across the entrance to the tomb and departed" (Matthew 27:60).

Hail Mary

Mary, Our Mother of Sorrows, pray for us.

~ Pray three Hail Mary's in honor of the tears Mary shed.

Prayer to Our Lady of Sorrows

O most holy Virgin, Mother of our Lord Jesus Christ: by the overwhelming grief you experienced when you witnessed the martyrdom, the crucifixion, and the death of your divine Son, look upon me with eyes of compassion, and awaken in my heart a tender commiseration for those sufferings, as well as a sincere detestation of my sins, in order that, being disengaged from all undue affection for the passing joys of this earth, I may sigh after the eternal Jerusalem, and that henceforward all my thoughts and all my actions may be directed towards this one most desirable object. Honor, glory, and love to our divine Lord Jesus, and to the holy and Immaculate Mother of God. Amen.

ST. BONAVENTURE

The Litany of the Sorrowful Mother

Lord, have mercy on us.
Christ, have mercy on us.
Lord, have mercy on us. Christ, hear us.
Christ, graciously hear us.
God the Father of Heaven,
have mercy on us.
God the Son, Redeemer of the world,
have mercy on us.
God the Holy Spirit,
have mercy on us.
Holy Trinity, one God,
have mercy on us.

Holy Mary, conceived without sin,
   pray for us. (Say this after each phrase below.)
Holy Mother of God,
Mother of Christ,
Mother of our Savior, Crucified,
Mother most sorrowful,
Mother most tearful,
Mother most afflicted,
Mother most lonely,
Mother most desolate,
Mother pierced by the sword of sorrow,

Queen of martyrs,
Comfort of the sorrowful,
Help of the needy,
Protectress of the forsaken,
Support of widows and orphans,
Health of the sick,
Hope of the troubled,
Haven of the ship-wrecked,
Refuge of sinners,
Hope of despairing,
Mother of mercy,

Through thy poverty in the stable of Bethlehem,
Through thy sorrow at the prophecy of Simeon,
Through thy sad flight into Egypt,
Through thy anxiety when seeking thy lost child,
Through thy grief when seeing thy Divine Son persecuted,
Through thy fear and anxiety when Jesus was apprehended,
Through the pain caused thee by the treason of Judas and the
      denial of Peter,

Through thy sad meeting with Jesus on the Way of the Cross,
Through the tortures thy loving Heart at the Crucifixion of Jesus,
Through thy agony at the death of Jesus,
Through the sword of sorrow that pierced thy heart when the side
of Jesus was transfixed by the lance,
Through thy lamentations over the dead Body of thy Divine Son
lying on thy bosom,
Through thy deep mourning at His tomb,
Through thy desolation after the burial of Jesus,
Through the tears thou didst shed for thy beloved Son,
Through thy wonderful resignation to the will of God in all thy
sufferings,

O Queen of peace,
In all our tribulations,
In our illnesses and pains,
In our sorrows and afflictions,
In our need and destitution,
In our fears and dangers,
In the hour of our death,
On the Day of Judgment,

Lamb of God, Who takest away the sins of the world,
spare us, O Lord.
Lamb of God, Who takest away the sins of the world,
graciously hear us, O Lord.
Lamb of God, Who takest away the sins of the world,
have mercy on us.

Pray for us, O Sorrowful Virgin,
That we may be made worthy of the promises of Christ.

Let us pray.

We beseech Thee, O Lord Jesus Christ, let Thy Mother, the Blessed Virgin Mary, whose holy soul was pierced by a sword of sorrow at the hour of Thy Passion, implore Thy mercy for us, both now and at the hour of our death, Who livest and reignest, world without end. Amen.

> ~ *The Catholic Church celebrates the*
> *Feast of Our Lady of Sorrows on September 15.*

THE CHAPLET OF THE
MOST PRECIOUS BLOOD

Almighty Father, I place the Precious Blood of Jesus
before my lips before I pray, that my prayers may be purified
before they ascend to Your divine Altar.

ST. MARY MAGDALENE DE PAZZI

The Chaplet of the Most Precious Blood consists of seven mysteries meditating on the seven times our Lord Jesus Christ shed his blood for us. The chaplet begins with the opening invocation and one Glory Be. The Our Father is said five times after each mystery except for the last, where it is said three times. The Glory Be is said once after each mystery in thanksgiving for the gift of the Most Precious Blood. In all, thirty-three Our Fathers are said in honor of the thirty-three years of the life of our Lord Jesus Christ on earth. The chaplet concludes with the closing Precious Blood prayer.

THE PRAYERS OF THE
CHAPLET OF THE MOST PRECIOUS BLOOD

O God, Come to my assistance,
O Lord, make haste to help me.

Glory be to the Father, the Son, and the Holy Spirit;
as it was in the beginning, is now, and ever shall be,
world without end. Amen.

The First Mystery

The first time our loving Savior shed his precious blood for us was
on the eighth day after his birth, when he was circumcised in order
to fulfill the law of Moses. While, then, we reflect that Jesus did this
to satisfy the justice of God for our lax ways, let us rouse ourselves
to sorrow for them, and promise, with the help of his all-powerful
grace, to be henceforth truly chaste in body and in soul.

Five Our Fathers, One Glory Be

We beseech Thee, therefore,
help thy servants, whom Thou
hast redeemed with thy Precious Blood.

The Second Mystery

Next, in the Garden of Olives, Jesus shed his blood for us in such
quantity that it bathed the earth around. He did this at the sight of
the ingratitude with which men would meet his love. Let us, then,
repent sincerely that we have hitherto corresponded so ill with the
countless blessings of God.

Five Our Fathers, One Glory Be

We beseech Thee, therefore,
help thy servants, whom Thou
hast redeemed with thy Precious Blood.

The Third Mystery

Next, in the cruel scourging, Jesus shed his blood when his flesh was so torn that streams of blood flowed from every part of his body, all of which he offered all the time to his eternal Father in payment of our impatience and our softness. How comes it, then, that we do not curb our anger and love of self? Henceforth, we will try our best to bear our troubles well, and, despising self, take peacefully the injuries which men may do us.

Five Our Fathers, One Glory Be

We beseech Thee, therefore,
help thy servants, whom Thou
hast redeemed with thy Precious Blood.

The Fourth Mystery

Again, from the sacred head of Jesus, blood poured down when it was crowned with thorns, in punishment of our pride and evil thoughts. Shall we, then, continue to nurture haughtiness, foster foul imaginations, and feed the wayward will within us? Henceforth, let there be ever before our eyes our utter nothingness, our misery, and our weakness; and with generous hearts let us resist all the temptations of the devil.

Five Our Fathers, One Glory Be

We beseech Thee, therefore,
help thy servants, whom Thou
hast redeemed with thy Precious Blood.

The Fifth Mystery

What streams of precious blood did not our loving Lord pour forth from his veins when laden with the heavy cross on that most grievous journey to Calvary! The very streets and ways of Jerusalem, through which he passed, were watered with it! This he did in satisfaction for the scandals and bad example by which his own creatures had led others astray. Who can tell how many of us are of this unhappy number? Who know how many he himself alone has, by his own bad example, brought down to hell? And what have we done to remedy this evil? Henceforth, let us at least do all we can to save souls by word and by example, making ourselves a pattern to all of goodness and a holy life.

Five Our Fathers, One Glory Be

> *We beseech Thee, therefore,*
> *help thy servants, whom Thou*
> *hast redeemed with thy Precious Blood.*

The Sixth Mystery

More, and still more precious blood did the Redeemer of mankind shed in his barbarous crucifixion; when, his veins being rent and arteries burst, there rushed forth in a torrent, from his hands and his feet, that saving balm of life eternal, to pay for all the crimes and enormities of a lost world. Who, after this, would continue in sin, and so renew the cruel crucifixion of the Son of God? Let us weep bitterly for our bad deeds done and detest them before the feet of the sacred minister of God. Let us amend our evil ways and henceforth begin a truly Christian life, with the remembrance ever in our hearts of all the blood which our salvation cost the Savior of men.

Five Our Fathers, One Glory Be

We beseech Thee, therefore,
help thy servants, whom Thou
hast redeemed with thy Precious Blood.

The Seventh Mystery

Last of all, after his death, when his sacred side was opened by the lance, and his loving heart was wounded, Jesus shed blood, and with it there came forth water, to show us how his blood was all poured out to the last drop for our salvation. Oh, the great goodness of our redeeming Lord! Who will not love thee, Savior of my soul? What heart will not consume itself away for love of thee, who hast done all this for our redemption? The tongue wants words to praise thee; so let us invite all creatures upon earth, all angels and all saints in paradise, and most of all our dear Mother Mary, to bless, praise, and celebrate thy most precious blood. Glory to the blood of Jesus! Glory to the blood of Jesus! Now and ever throughout all ages. Amen.

Three Our Fathers, One Glory Be

We beseech Thee, therefore,
help thy servants, whom Thou
hast redeemed with thy Precious Blood.

Most Precious Blood of life eternal! Price and ransom of the world! Drink and bathe of the soul! Ever leading the cause of man before the throne of Mercy; I adore Thee most profoundly; I would, if I were able, make Thee some compensation for the outrages and wrongs Thou dost ever suffer from men, and especially from those who dare in their rashness to blaspheme Thee. Who will not bless this Blood of value infinite? Who does not feel himself on fire with love of Jesus, who shed it all for us? What should I be but for this Blood, which hath redeemed me? And what drew Thee, Thou Precious

Blood, from the veins of my Lord, even to the last drop? It was love. O boundless love, which gave to us this saving balsam! O balsam beyond all price, streaming forth from the Fount of immeasurable love! Give to all hearts, all tongues, power to praise, celebrate, and thank Thee, now and ever, and throughout all eternity. Amen.

Thou hast redeemed us, O Lord, with thy Blood.
And hast made us a kingdom to our God.

Let us pray.

Almighty and everlasting God, who hast appointed thine only be-gotten Son the Savior of the world, and hast willed to be appeased by his Blood; grant us, we beseech Thee, so to venerate this Blood, the price of our salvation, and so to be defended on earth by its power from the evils of this present life, that in heaven we may be made glad by its everlasting fruit. Who liveth and reigneth, forever and ever. Amen.

****

Rest in Christ's Passion and live willingly in His Holy Wounds.
You will gain marvelous strength and comfort in adversities.

THOMAS À KEMPIS, *THE IMITATION OF CHRIST*

****

Prayer to the Shoulder Wound of Our Lord Jesus

O most loving Jesus, meek Lamb of God, I, a miserable sinner salute and worship the most Sacred Wound of Thy Shoulder on which Thou didst bear Thy heavy Cross, which so tore Thy Flesh and laid bare Thy Bones as to inflict on Thee an anguish greater than any other wound of Thy Most Blessed Body. I adore Thee, O Jesus, most sorrowful; I praise and glorify Thee, and give Thee thanks for this most sacred and painful Wound, beseeching Thee by that exceeding pain, and by the crushing burden of Thy heavy Cross, to be merciful to me, a sinner, to forgive me all my mortal and venial sins, and to lead me on towards Heaven along the Way of thy Cross. Amen.

~Pray one Our Father and three Hail Marys in honor of the wound where Christ shouldered the Cross.

*Holy Mother, imprint in my heart
The wounds of the crucified Jesus Christ.*

My Jesus, pardon and mercy through the merits of Thy Sacred Wounds.

Eternal Father I offer Thee the Wounds of our Lord Jesus Christ to heal the wounds of our souls.

The Litany of the Most Precious Blood of Jesus

Lord, have mercy on us.
   Christ, have mercy on us.
Lord, have mercy on us. Christ, hear us.
   Christ, graciously hear us.

God the Father of Heaven,
   have mercy on us.
God the Son, Redeemer of the world,
   have mercy on us.
God the Holy Spirit,
   have mercy on us.
Holy Trinity, One God,
   have mercy on us.

Blood of Christ, only begotten Son of the Eternal Father,
save us, (say this after each phrase below)
Blood of Christ, Incarnate Word of God,
Blood of Christ, of the New and Eternal Testament,
Blood of Christ, falling upon the earth in the Agony,
Blood of Christ, shed profusely in the Scourging,
Blood of Christ, flowing forth in the Crowning with Thorns,
Blood of Christ, poured out on the Cross,
Blood of Christ, Price of our salvation,
Blood of Christ, without which there is no forgiveness,
Blood of Christ, Eucharistic drink and refreshment of Souls,
Blood of Christ, river of Mercy,
Blood of Christ, Victor over demons,
Blood of Christ, Courage of Martyrs,
Blood of Christ, Strength of Confessors,
Blood of Christ, bringing forth Virgins,
Blood of Christ, Help of those in peril,
Blood of Christ, Relief of the burdened,
Blood of Christ, Solace in sorrow,
Blood of Christ, Hope of the penitent,
Blood of Christ, Consolation of the dying,
Blood of Christ, Peace and Tenderness of hearts,
Blood of Christ, Pledge of Eternal Life,
Blood of Christ, freeing souls from Purgatory,
Blood of Christ, most worthy of all glory and honor,

Lamb of God, who takest away the sins of the world,
spare us, O Lord.
Lamb of God, who takest away the sins of the world,
graciously hear us, O Lord.

Lamb of God, who takest away the sins of the world,
   have mercy on us.

Thou hast redeemed us, O Lord, in Thy Blood,
   And made of us a kingdom for our God.

   Let us pray.

Almighty and Eternal God, Thou hast appointed Thine only be-gotten Son the Redeemer of the world, and willed to be appeased by His Blood. Grant, we beseech Thee, that we may worthily adore this Price of our salvation, and through its power be safeguarded from the evils of this present life, so that we may rejoice in its fruits forever in Heaven. Through the same Christ our Lord. Amen.

~ *Our Lord Jesus Christ said to St. Elizabeth, Queen of Hungry;*
St. Matilda; and St. Bridget:

For all the faithful to pray each day two Our Fathers,
two Hail Marys and two Glory Be's in honor of
the drops of Blood lost during His Passion.

~ *The Catholic Church dedicates the month of July to the*
Most Precious Blood of Our Lord Jesus Christ.

CATHOLIC PRAYERS

O Lord, you will open my lips,
and my mouth will proclaim your praise.
PSALM 51:17

MORNING PRAYERS

The Sign of the Cross

In the name of the Father,
and of the Son,
and of the Holy Spirit.
Amen.

> LORD, *in the morning you will hear my voice;*
> *in the morning I will plead before you and wait.*
> PSALM 5:3–4

The Glory Be (The Doxology)

Glory be to the Father, the Son, and the Holy Spirit;
as it was in the beginning, is now, and ever shall be,
world without end.
Amen.

Traditional Morning Offering

O Jesus, through the Immaculate Heart of Mary, I offer You my prayers, works, joys and sufferings of this day in union with the Holy Sacrifice of the Mass throughout the world. I offer them for all the intentions of Your Sacred Heart: the salvation of souls, reparation for sin, and the reunion of all Christians. I offer them for the intentions of our bishops and of all Apostles of Prayer, and in particular for those recommended by our Holy Father this month.

APOSTLESHIP OF PRAYER

Morning Offering

My most sweet Lord, I offer and consecrate to you this morning all that I am and have; my thoughts, my senses, my affections, my desires, my pleasures, my inclinations, my liberty. In a word, I place my whole body and soul in your hands.

ST. ALPHONSUS LIGUORI

Secret of Sanctity Prayer

~ As I begin this day I pray ...

O Holy Spirit, beloved of my soul, I adore You. Enlighten me, guide me, strengthen me, console me. Tell me what I should do; give me your orders. I promise to submit myself to all that You desire of me and accept all that You permit to happen to me. Let me only know Your Will.

JOSEPH CARDINAL MERCIER

PRAYERS TO THE HOLY TRINITY

To the one who sits on the throne and to the Lamb
be blessing and honor, glory and might,
forever and ever.
REVELATION 5:13

Prayer to the Blessed Trinity

The Father is my hope.
The Son is my refuge.
The Holy Spirit is my protector.
Glory to the holy and undivided Trinity,
now and forever.

Let us Praise the Father,
the Son and the Holy Spirit;
let us bless and exalt God above all forever!

Almighty and everlasting God,
to whom we owe the grace of professing the true faith,
grant that while acknowledging the glory of the eternal Trinity
and adoring its unity,
we may through Your majestic power
be confirmed in this faith
and defended against all adversities;
through Jesus Christ our Lord,
who lives and reigns with You
in the unity of the Holy Spirit, one God,
forever and ever.
Amen.

Prayer to the Holy Trinity

Glory be to the Father, who by His almighty power and love created me, making me in the image and likeness of God.

Glory be to the Son, who by his Precious Blood delivered me from hell, and opened for me the gates of heaven.

Glory be to the Holy Spirit, who has sanctified in the sacrament of Baptism, and continues to sanctify me by the graces I receive daily from His bounty.

Glory be to the Three adorable Persons of the Holy Trinity, now and forever. Amen.

Te Deum

You are God: we praise you;
You are the Lord: we acclaim you;
You are the eternal Father: All creation worships you.

To you all angels, all the powers of heaven,
Cherubim and Seraphim, sing in endless praise:

> Holy, holy, holy, Lord, God of power and might,
> heaven and earth are full of your glory.

The glorious company of apostles praise you.
The noble fellowship of prophets praise you,
The white-robed army of martyrs praise you.

Throughout the world the holy Church acclaims you:

> Father, of majesty unbounded,
> your true and only Son, worthy of all worship,
> and the Holy Spirit, advocate, and guide.

You, Christ, are the king of glory,
the eternal Son of the Father.
When you became man to set us free
you did not spurn the Virgin's womb.
You overcame the sting of death,
and opened the kingdom of heaven to all believers.
You are seated at God's right hand in glory.
We believe that you will come, and be our judge.
Come then, Lord, and help your people,
bought with the price of your own blood,
and bring us with your saints to glory everlasting.

Save your people, Lord, and bless your inheritance.
Govern and uphold them now and always.

Day by day we bless you.
We praise your name for ever.

Keep us today, Lord, from all sin.
Have mercy on us, Lord, have mercy.

Lord, show us your love and mercy;
for we put our trust in you.

In you, Lord is our hope:
and we shall never hope in vain.

Renewal of Baptismal Promises

Do you reject sin so as to live in the freedom of God's children?
   I do.
Do you reject the glamour or evil and refuse to be mastered by sin?
   I do.
Do you reject Satan, father of sin and prince of darkness?
   I do.
Do you believe in God, the Father Almighty, creator of heaven and earth?
   I do.
Do you believe in Jesus Christ, His only Son our Lord, who was born of the Virgin Mary, was crucified, died, and was buried, rose from the dead, and is now seated at the right hand of the Father?
   I do.
Do you believe in the Holy Spirit, the holy Catholic Church, the communion of saints, the forgiveness of sins, the resurrection of the body, and life everlasting?
   I do.
This is our faith. This is the faith of the Church. We are proud to profess it in Christ Jesus our Lord.
Amen.

PRAYERS TO GOD THE FATHER

I will extol you, my God and king;
I will bless your name forever and ever.
Every day I will bless you;
I will praise your name forever and ever.
PSALM 145:1–2

Act of Faith

O my God, I firmly believe that You are one God in three Divine Persons, Father, Son, and Holy Spirit. I believe that Your divine Son became man, died for our sins, and that He will come to judge the living and the dead. I believe these and all the truths which the Holy Catholic Church teaches because You have revealed them, who can neither deceive nor be deceived. Amen.

Act of Hope

O my God, relying on Your infinite goodness and promises, I hope to obtain pardon for my sins, the help of Your grace and life everlasting, through the merits of Jesus Christ, my Lord and Redeemer. Amen.

Act of Love

O my God, I love You above all things, with my whole heart and soul, because You are all good and worthy of all my love. I love my neighbor as myself for the love of You. I forgive all who have injured me, and ask pardon for all whom I have injured. Amen.

Psalm 63:2–9

O God, you are my God—
it is you I seek!
For you my body yearns;
for you my soul thirsts,
In a land parched, lifeless,
and without water.
I look to you in the sanctuary
to see your power and glory.
For your love is better than life;
my lips shall ever praise you!
I will bless you as long as I live;
I will lift up my hands, calling on your name.
My soul shall be sated as with choice food,
with joyous lips my mouth shall praise you!
I think of you upon my bed,
I remember you through the watches of the night
You indeed are my savior,
and in the shadow of your wings I shout for joy.
My soul clings fast to you;
your right hand upholds me.

Litany of the Love of God

Lord, have mercy on us.
Christ, have mercy on us.
Lord, have mercy on us. Christ, hear us.
Christ, graciously hear us.
God the Father of Heaven,
have mercy on us.
God the Son, Redeemer of the world,
have mercy on us.

God the Holy Spirit,
have mercy on us.
Holy Trinity, One God,
have mercy on us.

Thou Who are Infinite Love,
I love Thee, O my God. (Say this after each phrase below.)
Thou Who didst first love me,
Thou Who dost command me to love Thee,

> with all my heart,
> with all my soul,
> with all my mind,
> with all my strength,

above all possessions and honor,
above all pleasures and enjoyments,
more than myself and all that belongs to me,
more than all my relatives and friends,
more than all men and angels,
above all created things in Heaven or on earth,
only for Thyself,

because Thou art the sovereign Good,
because Thou art infinitely worthy of being loved,
because Thou art infinitely perfect,

even hadst Thou not promised me Heaven,
even hadst Thou not menaced me with Hell,
even shouldst Thou try me by want and misfortune,

in wealth and in poverty,
in prosperity and in adversity,
in health and in sickness,
in life and in death,
in time and in eternity,

in union with that love wherewith all the Saints and
all the Angels love Thee in Heaven,
in union with that love wherewith the Blessed Virgin Mary
loveth Thee,
in union with that infinite love wherewith
Thou lovest Thyself eternally.

Let us pray.

My God, Who dost possess in incomprehensible abundance all that is perfect and worthy of love, annihilate in me all guilty, sensual, and undue love for creatures; kindle in my heart the pure flame of Thy love, so that I may love nothing but Thee or in Thee, until, being entirely consumed by holy love of Thee, I may go to love Thee eternally with the elect in Heaven, the country of pure love. Amen.

POPE PIUS VI

PRAYERS TO JESUS

The LORD, my strength and might,
has become my savior.
PSALM 118:14

Prayer to the Sacred Heart of Jesus

O Most Sacred Heart of Jesus, fountain of every blessing. I adore You, I love You and with true sorrow for my sins, I offer You this poor heart of mine. Make me humble, patient, pure, and wholly obedient to Your will. Grant, good Jesus, that I may live in You and for You. Protect me in the midst of danger, comfort me in my afflictions, give me health of body, assistance in my temporal needs, Your blessing on all that I do, and the grace of a holy death. Amen.

Novena to the Sacred Heart of Jesus

O my Jesus, you have said, "Truly I say to you, ask and it will be given to you, seek and you will find, knock and it will be opened to you." Behold, I knock, I seek, and I ask for the grace of—

Our Father, Hail Mary, Glory Be

Sacred Heart of Jesus, I place all my trust in You.

O my Jesus, You have said, "Truly I say to you, if you ask anything of the Father in my name, He will give it to you." Behold, in Your name, I ask the Father for the grace of—

Our Father, Hail Mary, Glory Be

Sacred Heart of Jesus, I place all my trust in You.

O my Jesus, You have said, "Truly I say to you, heaven and earth will pass away, but My words will not pass away." Encouraged by Your infallible words, I now ask for the grace of—

Our Father, Hail Mary, Glory Be

Sacred Heart of Jesus, I place all my trust in You.

Let us pray.

O Sacred Heart of Jesus, for Whom it is impossible not to have compassion on the afflicted, have pity on us poor sinners and grant us the grace which we ask of You, through the Sorrowful and Immaculate heart of Mary, Your tender Mother and ours. Amen. Hail, Holy Queen

St. Joseph, foster father of Jesus, pray for us.
ST. PADRE PIO PRAYED THIS PRAYER EVERY DAY FOR OTHERS.

****

Jesus meek and humble of heart,
make my heart like unto Thine.

****

Consecration Prayer to the Sacred Heart of Jesus

O Sacred Heart of Jesus, filled with infinite love, broken by my ingratitude, pierced by my sins, yet loving me still; accept the consecration that I make to You, of all that I am and all that I have. Take every faculty of my soul and body. Draw me, day by day, nearer and nearer to Your Sacred Heart, and there, as I can understand the lesson, teach me Your blessed ways. Amen.

Litany of the Most Sacred Heart of Jesus

Lord, have mercy on us.
  Christ, have mercy on us.
Lord, have mercy on us. Christ, hear us.
  Christ, graciously hear us.
God the Father of Heaven,
  have mercy on us.
God the Son, Redeemer of the world,
  have mercy on us.
God the Holy Spirit,
  have mercy on us.
Holy Trinity, one God,
  have mercy on us.

Heart of Jesus, Son of the Eternal Father,
  have mercy on us. (Say this after each phrase below.)
Heart of Jesus, formed by the Holy Spirit
          in the womb of the Virgin Mother,
Heart of Jesus, substantially united to the Word of God,
Heart of Jesus, of infinite majesty,
Heart of Jesus, holy Temple of God,
Heart of Jesus, Tabernacle of the Most High,
Heart of Jesus, House of God and Gate of heaven,
Heart of Jesus, burning Furnace of charity,
Heart of Jesus, Vessel of justice and love,
Heart of Jesus, full of goodness and love,
Heart of Jesus, abyss of all virtues,
Heart of Jesus, most worthy of all praise,
Heart of Jesus, King and center of all hearts,
Heart of Jesus, in whom are all the treasures of wisdom
          and knowledge,

Heart of Jesus, in whom dwelleth all the fullness of the divinity,
Heart of Jesus, in whom the Father was well pleased,
Heart of Jesus, of whose fullness we have all received,
Heart of Jesus, desire of the everlasting hills,
Heart of Jesus, patient and abounding in mercy,
Heart of Jesus, rich unto all who call upon Thee,
Heart of Jesus, Fountain of life and holiness,
Heart of Jesus, Propitiation for our sins,
Heart of Jesus, filled with reproaches,
Heart of Jesus, bruised for our offenses,
Heart of Jesus, made obedient unto death,
Heart of Jesus, pierced with a lance,
Heart of Jesus, Source of all consolation,
Heart of Jesus, our Life and Resurrection,
Heart of Jesus, our Peace and Reconciliation,
Heart of Jesus, Victim for our sins,
Heart of Jesus, Salvation of those who hope in Thee,
Heart of Jesus, Hope of those who die in Thee,
Heart of Jesus, Delight of all the saints,

Lamb of God, who takest away the sins of the world,
spare us, O Lord.
Lamb of God, who takest away the sins of the world,
graciously hear us, O Lord.
Lamb of God, who takest away the sins of the world,
have mercy on us.

> *Jesus meek and humble of heart,*
> *make my heart like unto Thine.*

Let us pray.

Almighty and eternal God, consider the Heart of Thy well-beloved Son and the praises and satisfaction He offers Thee in the name of sinners; appeased by worthy homage, pardon those who implore Thy mercy, in the name of the same Jesus Christ, Thy Son, Who lives and reigns with Thee, world without end. Amen.

~ Glory, love and thanksgiving be to the Sacred Heart of Jesus! ~

Short Aspirations to Jesus

Merciful Jesus,
I consecrate myself today and always to Thy Most Sacred Heart.
Most Sacred Heart of Jesus I implore,
that I may ever love Thee more and more.
Most Sacred Heart of Jesus, I trust in Thee.
Most Sacred Heart of Jesus, I unite all my sufferings to Thine.
Sacred Heart of Jesus, I believe in Thy love for me.
Sacred Heart of Jesus, Thy Kingdom come.
My Jesus, save me!
My Jesus, mercy!
Jesus, I love you!
Jesus.

> *I thank you, Lord, with all my heart;*
> *in the presence of the angels to you I sing.*
> *I bow low toward your holy temple;*
> *I praise your name for your mercy and faithfulness.*
> PSALM 138:1–2

The Divine Praises

Blessed be God.
Blessed be His Holy Name.
Blessed be Jesus Christ, true God and true man.
Blessed be the Name of Jesus.
Blessed be His Most Sacred Heart.
Blessed be His most precious Blood.
Blessed be Jesus in the Most Holy Sacrament of the Altar.
Blessed be the Holy Spirit, the Paraclete.
Blessed be the great Mother of God, Mary most holy.
Blessed be her holy and Immaculate Conception.
Blessed be Her glorious Assumption.
Blessed be the name of Mary, Virgin and Mother.
Blessed be St. Joseph, her most chaste spouse.
Blessed be God in His angels and in His Saints.

May the heart of Jesus, in the Most Blessed Sacrament, be praised, adored, and loved with grateful affection, at every moment, in all the tabernacles of the world, even to the end of time. Amen.

A Spiritual Communion

O Jesus, I turn toward the Holy Tabernacle where You live hidden for love of me. I love you, O my God. I cannot receive You in Holy Communion. Come nevertheless and visit me with your grace. Come spiritually into my heart. Purify it, sanctify it, render it like unto Your own. Amen.

Lord, I am not worthy that you should enter under my roof, but only say the word and my soul shall be healed.

May the Body and Blood of Our Lord Jesus Christ bring me to everlasting life.

Anima Christi

Soul of Christ, sanctify me.
Body of Christ, save me.
Blood of Christ, inebriate me.
Water from the side of Christ, wash me.
Passion of Christ, strengthen me.
O good Jesus, hear me.
Within your wounds conceal me.
Do not permit me to be parted from you.
From the evil foe protect me.
At the hour of my death call me.
And bid me come to you,
to praise you with all your saints
for ever and ever.
Amen.

Stay with me, Lord

Stay with me, Lord, for it is necessary to have you present so that I
        do not forget You.
You know how easily I abandon You.

Stay with me, Lord, because I am weak and I need Your strength,
        that I may not fall so often.
Stay with me Lord, for You are my life, and without You, I am
        without fervor.

Stay with me, Lord, for You are my light, and without You, I am
        in darkness.
Stay with me, Lord, to show me Your will.
Stay with me, Lord, so that I can hear Your voice and follow You.

Stay with me, Lord, for I desire to love You very much, and always be in Your company.

Stay with me, Lord, if You wish me to be faithful to You.

Stay with me, Lord, for as poor as my soul is, I want it to be a place of consolation for You, a nest of love.

Stay with me, Jesus, for it is getting late and the day is coming to a close and life passes; death, judgment, eternity approaches.

It is necessary to renew my strength, so that I will not stop along the way and for that, I need You.

It is getting late and death approaches, I fear the darkness, the temptations, the dryness, the cross, the sorrows. Oh how I need You, my Jesus, in the night of exile!

Stay with me tonight, Jesus, in life with all its dangers. I need You.

Let me to recognize You as Your disciples did at the breaking of the bread, so that the Eucharistic Communion be the light which disperses the darkness, the force which sustains me, the unique joy of my heart.

Stay with me, Lord, because at the hour of my death, I want to remain united to You, if not by communion, at least by grace and love.

Stay with me, Jesus, I do not ask for divine consolation, because I do not merit it, but the gift of Your Presence,

Oh yes! I ask this of You!

Stay with me, Lord, for it is You alone I look for, Your Love, Your Grace, Your Will, Your Heart, Your Spirit because I love You and ask no other reward but to love You more and more.

*With a firm love, I will love You with all my heart while on earth
and continue to love You perfectly during all eternity.*

ST. PADRE PIO OF PIETRELCINA
THIS PRAYER IS KNOWN AS PADRE PIO'S PRAYER AFTER HOLY COMMUNION.

Prayer of Adoration

I adore Thee, O Jesus, true God and true Man, here present in the
Holy Eucharist, humbly kneeling before Thee and united in spirit
with all the faithful on earth and all the blessed in heaven. In deepest gratitude for so great a blessing, I love Thee, my Jesus, with my
whole heart, for Thou art all perfect and all worthy of love. Give me
grace nevermore in any way to offend Thee, and grant that I being
refreshed by Thy Eucharistic presence here on earth, may be found
worthy to come to the enjoyment with Mary of Thine eternal and
ever blessed presence in heaven. Amen.

Psalm 34:2–21

I will bless the LORD at all times;
his praise shall be always in my mouth.
My soul will glory in the LORD;
let the poor hear and be glad.

Magnify the LORD with me;
and let us exalt his name together.
I sought the LORD, and he answered me,
delivered me from all my fears.

Look to him and be radiant,
and your faces may not blush for shame.
This poor one cried out and the LORD heard,
and from all his distress he saved him.

The angel of the LORD encamps
around those who fear him, and he saves them.
Taste and see that the LORD is good;
blessed is the stalwart one who takes refuge in him.

Fear the LORD, you his holy ones;
nothing is lacking to those who fear him.
The rich grow poor and go hungry,
but those who seek the LORD lack no good thing.

Come, children, listen to me;
I will teach you fear of the LORD.
Who is the man who delights in life,
who loves to see the good days?

Keep your tongue from evil,
your lips from speaking lies.
Turn from evil and do good;
seek peace and pursue it.

The eyes of the LORD are directed toward the righteous
and his ears toward their cry.
The LORD'S face is against evildoers
to wipe out their memory from the earth.

The righteous cry out, the LORD hears
and he rescues them from all their afflictions.
The LORD is close to the brokenhearted,
saves those whose spirit is crushed.

Many are the troubles of the righteous,
but the LORD delivers him from them all.
He watches over all his bones;
not one of them shall be broken.

The Golden Arrow Prayer

May the most holy, most sacred, most adorable, most incomprehensible and unutterable Name of God be always praised, blessed, loved, adored and glorified in Heaven, on earth, and under the earth, by all the creatures of God and by the Sacred Heart of Our Lord Jesus Christ, in the Most Holy Sacrament of the Altar. Amen.

Eternal Father, I offer Thee the adorable Face of Thy Beloved Son for the honor and glory of Thy Name, for the conversion of sinners and the salvation of the dying. Amen.

The Litany of the Holy Face of Jesus

I salute Thee, I adore Thee and I love Thee, O adorable Face of Jesus, my Beloved, noble Seal of the Divinity! Outraged anew by blasphemers, I offer Thee; through the heart of Thy blessed Mother, the worship of all the Angels and Saints, most humbly beseeching Thee to repair and renew in me and in all men Thy image disfigured by sin.

O adorable Face which was adored, with profound respect by
Mary and Joseph when they saw Thee for the first time,
have mercy on us.

O adorable Face which did ravish with joy, in the stable of
Bethlehem, the Angels, the shepherds and the Magi,
have mercy on us.

O adorable Face which transpierced with a dart of love in the
Temple, the saintly old man Simeon and the
prophetess Anna,
have mercy on us.

O adorable Face which filled with admiration the Doctors of the law when Thou appeared in the Temple at the age of twelve years,

have mercy on us.

O adorable Face which possesses beauty always ancient and always new,

have mercy on us.

O adorable Face which is the masterpiece of the Holy Ghost, in which the Eternal Father is well pleased,

have mercy on us.

O adorable Face which is the ineffable mirror of the divine perfections.

have mercy on us.

Adorable Face of Jesus which was so mercifully bowed down on the Cross, on the day of Thy Passion, for the salvation of the world! Once more today in pity bend down towards us poor sinners. Cast upon us a glance of compassion and give us Thy peace.

O adorable Face which became brilliant like the sun and radiant with glory, on the Mountain of Tabor,

have mercy on us.

O adorable Face which wept and was troubled at the tomb of Lazarus,

have mercy on us.

O adorable Face which was rendered sad at the sight of Jerusalem and shed tears on that ungrateful city,

have mercy on us.

O adorable Face which was bowed down to the ground in the Garden of Olives, and covered with confusion for our sins,

have mercy on us.

O adorable Face which was covered with the sweat of blood,

have mercy on us.

O adorable Face which was struck by a vile servant, covered with a veil of shame, and profaned by the sacrilegious hands of Thy enemies,

have mercy on us.

O adorable Face which by Its divine glance, wounded the heart of St. Peter with a dart of sorrow and love,

have mercy on us.

Be merciful to us, O my God! Do not reject our prayers, when in the midst of our afflictions, we call upon Thy Holy Name and seek with love and confidence Thy adorable Face.

O adorable Face which was washed and anointed by Mary and the holy women and covered with a shroud,

have mercy on us.

O adorable Face which was all resplendent with glory and beauty on the day of the Resurrection,

have mercy on us.

O adorable Face which is hidden in the Eucharist,

have mercy on us.

O adorable Face which will appear at the end of time in the clouds with great power and great majesty,

have mercy on us.

O adorable Face which will make sinners tremble,

have mercy on us.

O adorable Face which will fill the just with joy for all eternity,
   have mercy on us.
O adorable Face which merits all our reverence, our homage and
      our adoration,
   have mercy on us.
O Lord, show us Thy Face, and we shall be saved!
O Lord, show us Thy Face, and we shall be saved!
O Lord, show us Thy Face, and we shall be saved!
Amen.

> *Oh Jesus, through the merits of Your Holy Face,*
> *have pity on us, and on the whole world.*

SR. MARY OF ST. PETER

PRAYERS TO THE HOLY SPIRIT

> *And I will ask the Father,*
> *and he will give you another Advocate*
> *to be with you always, the Spirit of truth.*
> JOHN 14:16–17

Come Holy Spirit

Come, Holy Spirit, fill the hearts of Your faithful and enkindle in them the fire of Your love.

> *Send forth Your Spirit and they shall be created.*
> *And You shall renew the face of the earth.*

   Let us pray.

O God, who by the light of the Holy Spirit, did instruct the hearts of the faithful, grant us in the same Spirit to be truly wise and ever to rejoice in His consolation. Through Christ our Lord. Amen.

Act of Consecration to the Holy Spirit

On my knees before the great multitude of heavenly witnesses, I offer myself, soul and body, to You, Eternal Spirit of God. I adore the brightness of Your purity, the unerring keenness of Your justice, and the might of Your love. You are the Strength and Light of my soul. In You I live and move and am. I desire never to grieve You by unfaithfulness to grace and I pray with all my heart to be kept from the smallest sin against You. Mercifully guard my every thought and grant that I may always watch for Your light, and listen to Your voice, and follow Your gracious inspirations. I cling to You and give myself to You and ask You, by Your compassion, to watch over me in my weakness. Holding the pierced Feet of Jesus and looking at His Five Wounds, and trusting in His Precious Blood and adoring His opened Side and stricken Heart, I implore You, Adorable Spirit, Helper of my infirmity, to keep me in Your grace that I may never sin against You. Give me grace, O Holy Spirit, Spirit of the Father and the Son to say to You always and everywhere, "Speak Lord for Your servant heareth." Amen.

Prayer for the Seven Gifts of the Holy Spirit

O Lord Jesus Christ Who, before ascending into heaven did promise to send the Holy Spirit to finish Your work in the souls of Your Apostles and Disciples—deign to grant the same Holy Spirit to me, to perfect in my soul, the work of Your grace and Your love.

Grant me the Spirit of Wisdom—that I may not be attached to the perishable things of this world, but aspire only after the things that are eternal.

The Spirit of Understanding—to enlighten my mind with the light of Your divine truth.

The Spirit of Counsel—that I may ever choose the surest way of pleasing God and gaining heaven.

The Spirit of Fortitude—that I may bear my cross with You, and that I may overcome with courage all the obstacles that oppose my salvation.

The Spirit of Knowledge—that I may know God and know myself, and grow perfect in the science of the Saints.

The Spirit of Piety—that I may find the service of God sweet and amiable.

The Spirit of Fear—that I may be filled with a loving reverence towards God and may avoid anything that may displease Him.

Mark me, dear Lord, with the sign of Your true disciples, and animate me in all things with Your Spirit. Amen.

The fruit of the Spirit is love, joy, peace, patience, kindness, generosity, faithfulness, gentleness and self-control.

GALATIANS 5:22–23

Outpouring of the Holy Spirit

Holy Spirit, we ask for an outpouring of your graces, blessings and gifts upon those who do not believe, that they may believe; upon those who are doubtful or confused, that they may understand; upon those who are lukewarm or indifferent, that they may be transformed; upon those who are constantly living in the state of sin, that they may be converted; upon those who are weak, that may be strengthened; upon those who are holy, that they may persevere. Amen.

Prayer to the Holy Spirit

Breathe in me, O Holy Spirit, that my thoughts may all be holy.
Act in me, O Holy Spirit, that my work, too, may be holy.
Draw my heart, O Holy Spirit, that I may love but what is holy.
Strengthen me, O Holy Spirit, to defend all that is holy. Guard me,
then, O Holy Spirit, that I always may be holy. Amen.

ST. AUGUSTINE

Be filled with the Spirit, addressing one another in psalms
and hymns and spiritual songs singing and playing
to the Lord in your hearts.

EPHESIANS 5:18–19

Come Holy Spirit, Creator Blest—Veni, Creator Spiritus

Come, Holy Spirit, Creator blest,
and in our souls take up thy rest;
come with Thy grace and heavenly aid
to fill the hearts which Thou hast made.

O comforter, to Thee we cry,
O heavenly gift of God Most High,
O fount of life and fire of love,
and sweet anointing from above.
Thou in thy sevenfold gifts are known;
Thou, finger of God's hand we own;
Thou, promise of the Father, Thou
Who dost the tongue with power imbue.

Kindle our sense from above,
and make our hearts o'erflow with love;
with patience firm and virtue high
the weakness of our flesh supply.

Far from us drive the foe we dread,
and grant us Thy peace instead;
so shall we not, with Thee for guide,
turn from the path of life aside.

Oh, may Thy grace on us bestow
the Father and the Son to know;
and Thee, through endless times confessed,
of both the eternal Spirit blest.

Now to the Father and the Son,
Who rose from death, be glory given,
with Thou, O Holy Comforter,
henceforth by all in earth and heaven.
Amen.

Litany of the Holy Spirit

Lord, have mercy on us.
   Christ, have mercy on us.
Lord, have mercy on us. God the Father in Heaven,
   have mercy on us.
God the Son, Redeemer of the world,
   have mercy on us.
God the Holy Spirit,
   have mercy on us.
Holy Trinity, One God,
   have mercy on us.

Divine Essence, one true God,
   have mercy on us. (Say this after each phrase below.)
Spirit of truth and wisdom,
Spirit of holiness and justice,
Spirit of understanding and counsel,
Spirit of love and joy,
Spirit of peace and patience,
Spirit of long humility and meekness,
Spirit of benignity and goodness,

Love substantial of the Father and the Son,
Love and life of saintly souls,
Fire ever burning,
Living water to quench the thirst of hearts,

From all evil,
   deliver us, O Holy Spirit. (Say this after each phrase below.)
From all impurity of soul and body,
From all gluttony and sensuality,
From all attachments to the things of the earth,
From all hypocrisy and pretense,
From all imperfections and deliberate faults,
From all self-love and self-judgment,
From our own will,
From slander,
From deceiving our neighbors,
From our passions and disorderly appetites,
From our inattentiveness to Thy holy inspirations,
From despising little things,
From debauchery and malice,
From love of comfort and luxury,

From wishing to seek or desire anything other than Thee.
From everything that displeases Thee.

Most loving Father,
   forgive us.
Divine Word,
   have pity on us.
Holy and divine Spirit,
   leave us not until we are in possession of the Divine Essence,
   Heaven of heavens.

Lamb of God, Who takest away the sins of the world,
   send us the divine Consoler.
Lamb of God, Who takest away the sins of the world,
   fill us with the gifts of Thy Spirit.
Lamb of God, Who takest away the sins of the world,
   make the fruits of the Holy Spirit increase within us.

Come, O Holy Spirit, fill the hearts of Thy faithful,
   and enkindle in them the fire of Thy love.
Send forth Thy Spirit and they shall be created,
   and Thou shalt renew the face of the earth.

Let us pray.

O God, who by the light of the Holy Spirit didst instruct the hearts of the faithful, grant us by the same Spirit to be truly wise and ever to rejoice in His consolation. Through Jesus Christ our Lord. Amen.

THE HOLY FAMILY: PRAYERS TO JOSEPH

And Joseph was a righteous man.
MATTHEW 1:19

Prayer to St. Joseph

O, St. Joseph, whose protection is so great, so strong, so prompt before the throne of God, I place in thee all my interests and desires. O, St. Joseph, do assist me by thy powerful intercession, and obtain for me from thy Divine Son, Jesus Christ our Lord, all spiritual blessings, so that, having engaged here below thy heavenly power, I may offer my thanksgiving and homage to the most loving of Fathers. O, St. Joseph, I never weary of contemplating thee and Jesus asleep in thy arms; I dare not approach while He reposes near thy heart. Press Him in my name and kiss His fine head for me; and ask Him to return the kiss when I draw my dying breath.

St. Joseph, Patron of departing souls—Pray for me.
Amen.

Ave Joseph

Hail Joseph, filled with divine grace, in whose arms the Savior was carried and under whose eyes He grew up: blessed are thou among men and blessed is Jesus, the Son of thy dear Spouse.

Holy Joseph, chosen to be a father to the Son of God, pray for us in the midst of our cares of family, health and work, and deign to assist us at the hour of our death. Amen.

St. Joseph, father of Christ, is also your father and lord.
Ask him to help you.
ST. JOSEMARIA ESCRIVA

Prayer to St. Joseph

St. Joseph, our father and lord; most chaste, most pure. You were found worthy to carry the Child Jesus in your arms, to wash him, to hug him. Teach us to get to know God, and to be pure, worthy of being other Christs. And help us to do and to teach, as Christ did. Help us to open up the divine paths of the earth, which are both hidden and bright; and help us to show them to mankind, telling our fellow men that their lives on earth can have extraordinary and constant supernatural effectiveness.

ST. JOSEMARIA ESCRIVA, THE FORGE, NO. 553

Prayer of Consecration to St. Joseph

O blessed St. Joseph, I consecrate myself to thy honor, and give myself to thee, that thou mayest always be my father, my protector and my guide in the way of salvation. Obtain for me a great purity of heart and a fervent love of the interior life. After thy example may I do all my actions for the greater glory of God, in union with the Divine Heart of Jesus and the Immaculate Heart of Mary! And do thou, O Blessed St. Joseph, pray for me, that I may share in the peace and joy of thy holy death. Amen.

Prayer to St. Joseph for Protection

Gracious St. Joseph, protect me and my family from all evil as you did the Holy Family. Kindly keep us ever united in the love of Christ, ever fervent in imitation of the virtue of our Blessed Lady, your sinless spouse, and always faithful in devotion to you. Amen.

I know by experience,
that the glorious St. Joseph
assists us generally in all necessities.
I never asked him for anything which he did not obtain for me.

ST. TERESA OF ÁVILA

Memorare to St. Joseph

Remember, O most chaste Spouse of the Virgin Mary, that never has it been known that anyone who asked for thy help and sought thy intercession was left unaided. Full of confidence in thy power, I hasten to thee, and beg thy protection. Listen, O foster father of the Redeemer, to my humble prayer, and in thy goodness hear and answer me. Amen.

POPE PIUS IX

Prayer to St. Joseph, the Worker

O Joseph, model for all who labor, pray to God with us. It is an honor to use the gifts and develop the talents He has given us. May His grace strengthen us to work with order and patience, thankfulness, and joy. We pray that we may strive dutifully and conscientiously to fulfill our tasks, that all our accomplishments may benefit others and serve their needs. Then may the Lord crown our efforts at the hour of death, that we may join you in praising Him forever. Amen.

The Litany to St. Joseph

Lord, have mercy on us.
Christ, have mercy on us.
Lord, have mercy on us. Christ, hear us.
Christ, graciously hear us.

God the Father in heaven,
have mercy on us.
God the Son, Redeemer of the world,
have mercy on us.
God the Holy Spirit,
have mercy on us.
Holy Trinity, One God,
have mercy on us.

Holy Mary,
pray for us. (Say this after each phrase below.)
St. Joseph,
Illustrious son of David,
Light of patriarchs,
Spouse of the Mother of God,
Chaste guardian of the Virgin,
Foster-Father of the Son of God,
Watchful defender of Christ,
Head of the Holy Family,

Joseph most just,
Joseph most chaste,
Joseph most prudent,
Joseph most valiant,
Joseph most obedient,

Joseph most faithful,
Mirror of patience,
Lover of poverty,
Model of workmen,
Glory of domestic life,
Guardian of virgins,
Pillar of families,
Solace of the afflicted,
Hope of the sick,
Patron of the dying,
Terror of demons,
Protector of Holy Church,
Lamb of God, who takest away the sins of the world,
spare us, O Lord.
Lamb of God, who takest away the sins of the world,
graciously hear us, O Lord.
Lamb of God, who takest away the sins of the world,
have mercy on us.

He made him the lord of His household.
And prince over all His possessions.

Let us pray.

O God, Who in Thine ineffable providence didst choose Blessed
Joseph to be the spouse of Thy most Holy Mother, grant that as
venerate him as our protector on earth, we may deserve to have
him as our intercessor in Heaven, Thou Who livest and reignest
forever and ever. Amen.

St. Joseph, pray for us.

THE HOLY FAMILY: PRAYERS TO MARY

Then the Lord God said to the snake:
...I will put enmity between you and the woman,
and between your offspring and hers:
They will strike at your head.
<small>GENESIS 3:15</small>

The Magnificat

"My soul proclaims the greatness of the Lord;
my spirit rejoices in God my savior.
For he has looked upon his handmaid's lowliness;
behold, from now on will all ages call me blessed.
The Mighty One has done great things for me,
and holy is his name.

His mercy is from age to age
to those who fear him.
He has shown might with his arm,
dispersed the arrogant of mind and heart.

He has thrown down the rulers from their thrones
but lifted up the lowly.
The hungry he has filled with good things;
the rich he has sent away empty.

He has helped Israel his servant,
remembering his mercy,
according to his promise to our fathers,
to Abraham and to his descendants forever."

Glory to the Father, and to the Son, and to the Holy Spirit:
as it was in the beginning, is now, and will be forever. Amen.

Consecration to Mary

My Queen, my Mother,
I give myself entirely to you
and to show my devotion to you,
I consecrate to you this day,
my eyes, my ears, my mouth,
my heart, my whole being without reserve.
Wherefore good Mother as I am your own,
keep me, guard me as your property and possession.
Amen.

****

Live in Mary's heart,
love what she loves and desires.
Then you are sure to have peace, joy and holiness.
ST. JOHN EUDES

****

Affectionate Salutations to Mary

I greet thee, Mary Daughter of God the Father.
I greet thee, Mary, Mother of the Son of God.
I greet thee, Mary, Spouse of the Holy Spirit.

I greet thee, Mary, Temple of the Blessed Trinity.
I greet thee, Mary, White lily of the resplendent Trinity,
I greet thee, Mary, Fragrant Rose of the heavenly court.

I greet thee, Mary, Virgin full of meekness and humility of whom
the King of Heaven willed to be born and nourished by
thy milk.

I greet thee, Mary, Virgin of virgins.

I greet thee, Mary, Queen of martyrs, whose soul was pierced
by the sword of sorrow.
I greet thee, Mary, Lady and Mistress, to whom all power has been
given in heaven and earth.
I greet thee, Mary, Queen of my heart, my sweetness, my life and
my hope.
I greet thee, Mary, Mother most amiable.
I greet thee, Mary, Mother most admirable.
I greet thee, Mary, Mother of beautiful love.
I greet thee, Mary, Conceived without sin.

I greet thee, Mary, Full of grace, the Lord is with thee, blessed art
thou among women, and blessed be the Fruit of thy womb.

Blessed be thy spouse, St. Joseph.
Blessed be thy father, St. Joachim.
Blessed be thy mother, St. Anne.
Blessed be thy angel, St. Gabriel.

Blessed be the Eternal Father, Who has chosen thee.
Blessed be thy Son, Who has loved thee.
Blessed be thy Holy Spirit, Who has espoused thee.

May all those who love thee bless thee.
O Blessed Virgin, bless us all in the name of thy dear Son. Amen.

*~The original prayer begins each salutation with Hail Mary,
which was written by St. John Eudes.*

*Happy are those who love you,
and happy are those who rejoice in your peace.*

TOBIT 13:14

Sub Tuum Praesidium

~ The Church's oldest known prayer to our Lady:

We turn to you for protection,
Holy Mother of God.
Listen to our prayers
and help us in our needs.
Save us from every danger,
glorious and blessed Virgin.
Amen.

Mary, Help Those in Need

Holy Mary,
help those in need,
give strength to the weak,
comfort the sorrowful,
pray for God's people,
assist the clergy,
intercede for religious.
May all who seek your help
experience your unfailing protection.
Amen.

The Angelus

~ The Angelus is traditionally prayed at 6 a.m., noon, and 6 p.m. throughout the year, except during the Easter season.

The angel of the Lord declared unto Mary,
And she conceived by the Holy Spirit.

Hail Mary

Behold the handmaid of the Lord,
Be it done unto me according to Thy word.

Hail Mary

And the Word was made Flesh,
And dwelt among us.

Hail Mary

Pray for us, O holy Mother of God,
That we may be made worthy of the promises of Christ.

Let us pray.

Pour forth, we beseech Thee, O Lord, Thy grace into our hearts, that we, to whom the incarnation of Christ, Thy Son, was made known by the message of an angel, may by His Passion and Cross be brought to the glory of His Resurrection through the same Christ our Lord. Amen.

The Regina Coeli

~ Instead of the Angelus, *the* Regina Coeli *is prayed during the Easter season.*

Queen of Heaven, rejoice, alleluia.
   For He whom you did merit to bear, alleluia.
Has risen, as he said, alleluia.
   Pray for us to God, alleluia.
Rejoice and be glad, O Virgin Mary, alleluia.
   For the Lord has truly risen, alleluia.

   Let us pray.

O God, who gave joy to the world through the resurrection of Thy Son, our Lord Jesus Christ, grant we beseech Thee, that through the intercession of the Virgin Mary, His Mother, we may obtain the joys of everlasting life. Through the same Christ our Lord. Amen.

****

Mary is an echo of God,
speaking and repeating only God,
If you say "Mary," she says, "God."
ST. LOUIS DE MONTFORT

****

Prayer to Mary

O Mary, my Queen, I cast myself in the arms of your mercy. I place my soul and body in your blessed care and under your special protection today and everyday and above all at the hour of my departure from this world. I entrust to you all my hopes and consolations, all my anguish and misery, my life and the end of my life. Through your most holy intercession and through your merits, grant that all my works may be directed and carried out in accord with your will and the will of your Divine Son.

ST. LOUIS DE MONTFORT

Ancient Hymn to Mary

Mary the dawn, Christ the perfect day;
Mary the gate, Christ the heavenly way.

Mary the root, Christ the mystic vine;
Mary the grape, Christ the sacred wine.

Mary the wheat, Christ the living-bread;
Mary the stem, Christ the rose blood-red.

Mary the font, Christ the cleansing flood;
Mary the cup, Christ the Saving blood.

Mary the temple, Christ the temple's Lord;
Mary the shrine, Christ the God adored.

Mary the beacon, Christ the Haven's rest;
Mary the mirror, Christ the Vision Blest.

Mary the Mother, Christ the mother's Son;
By all things blest while endless ages run.

****

*Mary has a
most tender love for all of us.*

ST. ALPHONSUS LIGUORI

****

Prayer to Mary

Most holy Virgin Immaculate, my Mother Mary, to thee who art the Mother of my Lord, the Queen of the universe, the advocate, the hope, the refuge of sinners, I who am the most miserable of all sinners, have recourse this day.

I venerate thee, great Queen, and I thank thee for the many graces thou hast bestowed upon me even unto this day; in particular for having delivered me from the hell which I have so often deserved by my sins.

I love thee, most dear Lady; and for the love I bear thee, I promise to serve thee willingly for ever and to do what I can to make thee loved by others also. I place in thee all my hopes for salvation; accept me as thy servant and shelter me under thy mantle, thou who art the Mother of mercy. And since thou art so powerful with God, deliver me from all temptations, or at least obtain for me the strength to overcome them until death. From thee I implore a true love for Jesus Christ.

Through thee I hope to die a holy death. My dear Mother, by the love thou bearest to Almighty God, I pray thee to assist me always, but most of all at the last moment of my life. Forsake me not then, until thou shalt see me safe in heaven, there to bless thee and sing of thy mercies through all eternity. Such is my hope.

ST. ALPHONSUS LIGUORI

Our Lady of Good Hope

My Mother, My Confidence.

O Mary Immaculate, the precious name of Mother of Good Hope, with which I honor you, fills my heart to overflowing with the sweetest consolation and moves me to hope for every blessing from you. If such a title has been given to you, it is a sure sign that no one has recourse to you in vain. Accept, therefore, with a mother's love my devout homage, as I earnestly beseech you to be gracious to me in my every need. Above all I pray that you will make me live in constant union with you and your divine Son, Jesus. With you as my guide, I am certain that I shall walk in the right way; and that it will be my happy lot to hear you say on the last day of my life those words of comfort: "Come then, my good and faithful servant, enter into the joy of the Lord." Amen.

THE *RACCOLTA*, NO. 416

~ This prayer is also known as Our Lady of Confidence.

****

Never be afraid of loving the Blessed Virgin too much.
You can never love her more than Jesus did.
ST. MAXIMILIAN KOLBE

****

Totally Yours—Totus Tuus

Immaculate Conception, Mary, my Mother.
Live in me. Act in me. Speak in and through me.
Think your thoughts in my mind. Love through my heart.
Give me your dispositions and feelings.
Teach, lead and guide me to Jesus.

Correct, enlighten and expand my thoughts and behavior.
Possess my soul. Take over my entire personality and life,
Replace it with Yourself.
Incline me to constant adoration and thanksgiving,
Pray in me and through me.
Let me live in you and keep me in this union always.

ST. MAXIMILIAN KOLBE,
RECITED BY BLESSED POPE JOHN PAUL II

Consecration to the Immaculate Heart of Mary

O Mary, Virgin Most Powerful, and Mother of Mercy, Queen of Heaven, and Refuge of sinners, I consecrate myself to Your Immaculate Heart. I consecrate my being and my life, all that I have, all that I am, and all that I love. To You I give my body, my heart, and my soul. To you I give my home, my family, and my country. I desire everything in me, everything around me, belong to you.

To make this act of consecration purposeful and lasting I renew this day, at this time my promises of baptism. Finally, O Glorious Mother of God and loving Mother, I promise I shall try to inspire in others the devotion to you so as to hasten, through the Queenship of Your Immaculate Heart, the coming Kingdom of the Sacred Heart. Amen.

In dangers, in doubts, in difficulties,
think of Mary, call upon Mary.
Don't let her name depart from your lips;
never allow it to leave your heart. And that you may
more surely obtain the assistance of her prayer, don't
neglect to walk in her footsteps.

ST. BERNARD

The Memorare

Remember, O most gracious Virgin Mary, that never was it known that anyone who fled to thy protection, implored thy help, or sought thy intercession was left unaided. Inspired with confidence, I fly unto thee, O Virgin of virgins, my Mother. To thee do I come; before thee I stand, sinful and sorrowful. O Mother of the Word Incarnate, despise not my petitions, but in thy mercy hear and answer me. Amen.

ST. BERNARD

Prayer to Our Lady of Mount Carmel

O Most beautiful Flower of Mount Carmel,
Fruitful Vine,
splendor of Heaven,
Blessed Mother of the Son of God,
Immaculate Virgin,
assist me in this my necessity.
O Star of the sea,
help me and show me herein you are my Mother.

O Holy Mary,
Mother of God,
Queen of Heaven and Earth,
I humbly beseech you from the bottom of my heart,
to aid me in this necessity;
there are none that can withstand your power.
O show me herein you are my Mother.

O Mary, conceived without sin,
pray for us who have recourse to thee. (Repeat three times)

Sweet Mother,
   I place this cause in your hands. (Say this line three times.)

Prayer to Our Mother of Perpetual Help

See at your feet, O mother of Perpetual Help, a poor sinner who has recourse to you and confides in you. O Mother of Mercy, have pity on me! I hear you called the refuge and the hope of sinners; be my refuge and my hope. Help me, for the love of Jesus Christ; stretch forth your hand to a poor fallen creature who recommends herself/himself to you, and who devotes herself/himself to your service forever. I bless and thank Almighty God, who in His mercy has given me this confidence in you, which I hold to be a pledge of my eternal salvation. Mary, tender Mother, help. Mother of Perpetual Help, never allow me to lose my God. Amen.

****

I am your merciful Mother.
The Mother of all who love me,
of those who cry to me, of those who have confidence in me.

OUR LADY OF GUADALUPE

****

Prayer to Our Lady of Guadalupe

Holy Mary of Guadalupe, Mystical Rose, intercede for Holy Church, protect the Sovereign Pontiff, help all those who invoke you in their necessities; and since you are the ever Virgin Mary and Mother of the true God, obtain for us from your most holy Son the grace of keeping our faith, sweet hope in the midst of the bitterness of life, burning charity, and the precious gift of final perseverance. Amen.

Am I not here who am your Mother?
Are you not under my shadow and protection?
Am I not your fountain of Joy?
Are you not in the folds of my mantle?
In the crossing of my arms? Is there anything else you need?

OUR LADY OF GUADALUPE

Prayer to Our Lady of the Miraculous Medal

O Virgin Mother of God, Mary Immaculate, we dedicate and consecrate ourselves to you under the title of Our Lady of the Miraculous Medal. May this Medal be for each one of us a sure sign of your affection for us and a constant reminder of our duties towards you. Ever while wearing it, may we be blessed by your loving protection and preserved in the grace of your Son. O most powerful Virgin, Mother of our Savior, keep us close to you every moment of our lives. Obtain for us, your children, the grace of a happy death; so that, in union with you, we may enjoy the bliss of heaven forever. Amen.

O Mary, conceived without sin,
   pray for us who have recourse to you.
O Mary, conceived without sin,
   pray for us who have recourse to you.
O Mary, conceived without sin,
   pray for us who have recourse to you.

I am the Immaculate Conception.

OUR LADY OF LOURDES

Prayer to Our Lady of Lourdes

Immaculate Mary, you appeared to St. Bernadette and gave her a mission to build up Lourdes as a sacred shrine to bring people to God. Through Your intercession, countless graces have been given to the thousands of people who have flocked to Lourdes. Some have even received the grace of physical healing. I join my prayers to the pilgrims at your shrine who sing thousands of *Aves* to you. I place all my trust in you and give you all my love. Amen.

~ Our Lady of Lourdes, pray for us.

Immaculate Mary – Lourdes Hymn

Immaculate Mary, thy praises we sing;
who reignest in splendor with Jesus our King:
 Ave, ave, ave Maria.
 Ave, ave Maria.
In heaven the blessed thy glory proclaim;
on earth, we, thy children, invoke your sweet name.
 Ave, ave, ave Maria.
 Ave, ave Maria.
Thy name is our power, thy virtues our light,
thy love is our comfort, thy pleading our might.
 Ave, ave, ave Maria.
 Ave, ave Maria.
We pray for our mother, the Church upon earth;
and bless, Holy Mary, the land of our birth
 Ave, ave, ave Maria.
 Ave, ave Maria

My Immaculate Heart
will be your refuge and the way leading you to God.

OUR LADY OF FATIMA

Fatima Consecration to the Immaculate Heart of Mary

O Virgin Mary, most powerful Mother of Mercy, Queen of heaven and earth, in accordance with your wish made known at Fatima, I consecrate myself today to your Immaculate Heart. To you, I entrust all that I have, all that I am. Reign over me, dearest Mother, that I may be yours in prosperity and in adversity, in joy and in sorrow, in health and in sickness, in life and in death.

Most Compassionate Heart of Mary, Queen of Virgins, watch over my mind and my heart and preserve me from the deluge of impurity which you lamented so sorrowfully at Fatima. I want to be pure like you. I want to atone for the many crimes committed against Jesus and you. I want to call down upon this country and the whole world the peace of God in justice and charity. Mindful of this consecration, I now promise to strive to imitate you by the practice of the Christian virtues without regard for human respect. I resolve to receive Holy Communion of the first Saturday of every month when possible, and to offer daily five decades of the Rosary, with all my sacrifices in the spirit of penance and reparation. Amen.

FATIMA PRAYERS

The Pardon Prayer

O my God, I believe, I adore, I trust, and I love You! And I beg pardon for those who do not believe, do not adore, do not trust, and do not love You. Amen.

The Angel's Prayer

O Most Holy Trinity,
Father, Son, and Holy Spirit,
I adore You profoundly.
I offer You the most precious Body, Blood, Soul and Divinity
of Jesus Christ, present in all the tabernacles of the world, in
reparation for the outrages, sacrileges and indifferences by which
He is offended.
By the infinite merits of the Sacred Heart of Jesus and the
Immaculate Heart of Mary,
I beg the conversion of poor sinners. Amen.

The Eucharistic Prayer

Most Holy Trinity, I adore You!
My God, my God,
I love You in the Most Blessed Sacrament. Amen.

The Sacrifice Prayer

O My Jesus, it is for love of You, in reparation for the offenses committed against the Immaculate Heart of Mary, and for the conversion of poor sinners. Amen.

PRAYERS FOR THE POPE, PRIESTS, AND VOCATIONS

The harvest is abundant
but the laborers are few; so ask the master
of the harvest to send out laborers for his harvest.

LUKE 10:2

Prayer for the Pope

Lord, source of eternal life and truth, give to your shepherd, (Name of Pope) a spirit of courage and right judgment, a spirit of knowledge and love. By governing with fidelity those entrusted to his care may he, as successor to the Apostle of Peter and vicar of Christ, build Your Church into a sacrament of unity, love, and peace for all the world. We ask this through our Lord Jesus Christ, Your Son, Who lives and reigns with You and the Holy Spirit, one God, forever and ever. Amen.

Prayer for Priests

O Jesus, our great High Priest, hear my humble prayers on behalf of your priests. Give them a deep faith, a bright and firm hope and a burning love, which will ever increase in the course of their priestly life.

In their loneliness, comfort them. In their sorrows, strengthen them. In their frustrations, point out to them that it is through suffering that the soul is purified, and show them that they are needed by the Church; they are needed by souls; they are needed for the work of redemption.

O loving Mother Mary, Mother of Priests, take to your heart your sons who are close to you because of their priestly ordination and because of the power which they have received to carry on the work of Christ in a world which needs them so much. Be their comfort, be their joy, be their strength, and especially help them to live and to defend the ideals of consecrated celibacy.

JOHN CARDINAL CARBERRY

****

O Mary, Queen of the clergy,
pray for us;
obtain for us many holy priests.

****

Prayer for Missionaries

Lord Jesus Christ, watch over your missionaries—priests, religious, and lay people—who leave everything to give testimony to your word and your love. In difficult moments, sustain their energies, comfort their hearts, and crown their work with spiritual achievements. Let the adorable image of you crucified on the Cross, which accompanies them throughout life, speak to them of heroism, generosity, love and peace. Amen.

BLESSED POPE JOHN XXIII

For I know well the plans I have in mind
for you—oracle of the LORD—plans for your
welfare and not for woe, so as to give you a future of hope.

JEREMIAH 29:11

Prayer for Vocations

Jesus, High Priest and Redeemer forever, we beg you to call young men and women to your service as priests and religious. May they be inspired by the lives of dedicated priest, brothers, and sisters. Give to their parents the grace of generosity and trust toward you and their children so that their sons and daughters may be helped to choose their vocations in life with wisdom and freedom.

Lord, you told us that the harvest indeed is great but the laborers are few. Pray, therefore, the Lord of the harvest, to send laborers into his harvest. We ask that we may know and follow the vocation to which you have called us. We pray particularly for those called to serve as priests, brothers, and sisters; those whom you have called, those you are calling now, and those you will call in the future. May they be open and responsive to the call of serving your people. We ask this through Christ, our Lord. Amen.

THE ESSENTIAL CATHOLIC PRAYER BOOK, LIGUORI PUBLICATIONS

Prayer for Priestly Vocations

Father, in your plan for salvation you provide shepherds for your people. Fill your Church with the spirit of courage and love. Raise up worthy ministers for your altars and ardent but gentle servants of the gospel. Grant this through our Lord Jesus Christ, your Son, who lives and reigns with you and the Holy Spirit, one God, forever and ever. Amen.

THE ROMAN MISSAL

PRAYERS FOR THE FAMILY

Love is patient, love is kind.
It is not jealous, [love] is not pompous, it is not inflated,
it is not rude, it does not seek its own interests,
it is not quick-tempered, it does not brood over injury,
it does not rejoice over wrongdoing but rejoices with the truth.
It bears all things, believes all things, hopes all things,
endures all things.

1 CORINTHIANS 13:4–7

Blessing for Marriage

Almighty and eternal God, You have so exalted the unbreakable bond of marriage that it has become the sacramental sign of Your Son's union with the Church as His spouse.

Look with favor on us whom You have united with marriage as we ask for Your help and the protection of the Virgin Mary. We pray that in good times and in bad we will grow in love for each other; that we will resolve to be of one heart in the bond of peace.

Lord, in our struggles let us rejoice that You are near to help us; in our needs let us know that You are there to rescue us; in our joys let us see that You are the source of completion of every happiness. We ask this through Christ our Lord. Amen.

Prayer of Spouses for Each Other

Lord Jesus, grant that I and my spouse may have a true and understanding love for each other. Grant that we may both be filled with faith and trust. Give us the grace to live with each other in peace and harmony. May we always bear with one another's weaknesses and grow from each other's strengths. Help us to forgive one another's failings and grant us patience, kindness, cheerfulness, and the spirit of placing the well-being of one another ahead of self. May the love that brought us together grow and mature with each passing year. Bring us both ever closer to You through our love for each other. Let our love grow to perfection. Amen.

Prayer for My Family

O dear Jesus, I humbly implore You to grant Your special graces to our family. May our home be the shrine of peace, purity, love, labor and faith. I beg You, dear Jesus, to protect and bless all of us, absent and present, living and dead.

O Mary, loving Mother of Jesus, and our Mother, pray to Jesus for our family, for all the families of the world, to guard the cradle of the newborn, the schools of the young and their vocations.

Blessed Joseph, holy guardian of Jesus and Mary, assist us by your prayers in all the necessities of life. Ask of Jesus that special grace which He granted you, to watch over our home at the pillow of the sick and dying, so that with Mary and with you, heaven may find our family unbroken in the Sacred Heart of Jesus. Amen.

****

Jesus, Mary and St. Joseph,
I love you,
save souls.

****

Prayer for Our Youth

God, our Father, we thank You for the gift of love and the gift of life. We thank you for the gift of our children. We ask You to send Your holy angels to protect and guide them each day so that they will walk the narrow path of purity, self-control and obedience, as was taught to us by Your own Son, Jesus Christ. We ask this through Jesus Christ our Lord, in union with the Holy Spirit. Amen.

> *You formed my inmost being;*
> *you knit me in my mother's womb.*
> *I praise you, because I am wonderfully made;*
> *wonderful are your works!*
> *My very self you know.*
> PSALM 139:13–14

Prayer for the Unborn

Heavenly Father, You created mankind in Your own image and You desire that not even the least among us should perish. In Your love for us, You entrusted Your only Son to the Virgin Mary. Now, in Your love, protect against the wickedness of the evil, those little ones to whom You have given the gift of life. Amen.

Prayer to End Abortion

Lord God, I thank you today for the gift of my life, and for the lives of all my brothers and sisters. I know there is nothing that destroys more life than abortion, yet I rejoice that you have conquered death by the Resurrection of Your Son. I am ready to do my part in ending abortion. Today I commit myself never to be silent, never to be passive, never to be forgetful of the unborn. I commit myself to be active in the pro-life movement, and never to stop defending life until all my brothers and sisters are protected, and our nation once again becomes a nation with liberty and justice not just for some, but for all, through Christ our Lord. Amen!

PRIESTS FOR LIFE

Prayer to Defeat the Work of Satan

O Divine Eternal Father, in union with Your Divine Son and the Holy Spirit, and through the Immaculate Heart of Mary. I beg You to destroy the Power of Your greatest enemy—the evil spirits. Cast them into the deepest recesses of Hell and chain them forever! Take possession of Your Kingdom which You have created and which is rightfully Yours. Heavenly Father, give us the reign of the Sacred Heart of Jesus and the Immaculate Heart of Mary. I repeat this prayer out of pure love for You with every beat of my heart and with every breath I take. Amen.

PRAYERS TO KNOW THE WILL OF GOD

Trust in the LORD with all your heart,
on your own intelligence do not rely;
In all your ways be mindful of him,
and he will make straight your paths.

PROVERBS 3:5–6

Prayer to Know the Will of God

Lord, what is Your will that I do? I am completely open to Your plan for me. I desire to live only in You and to be guided by You forever. Grant that Your holy will may be carried out perfectly in me. Amen.

ST. JANE FRANCES DE CHANTAL

Prayer for Guidance

Lord, grant that I may always allow myself to be guided by You, always follow Your plans, and perfectly accomplish Your Holy Will. Grant that in all things, great and small, today and all the days of my life, I may do whatever You require of me. Help me to respond to the slightest prompting of Your Grace, so that I may be Your trustworthy instrument for Your honor. May Your Will be done in time and in eternity—by me, in me and through me. Amen.

ST. TERESA OF ÁVILA

Prayer Before Work

O Lord Jesus Christ, in union with Thy most perfect actions I commend to Thee this my work, to be directed according to Thy adorable will, for the salvation of all mankind. Amen.

ST. GERTRUDE THE GREAT

May the most just, the most high, the most lovable
Will of God be in all things done, praised and magnified forever!
Amen.

Prayer of Surrender

Take, O Lord, and receive my entire liberty, my memory, my understanding and my whole will. All that I am and all that I possess You have given me. I surrender it all to You to be disposed of according to Your will. Give me only Your love and Your grace; with these I will be rich enough, and will desire nothing more. Amen.

ST. IGNATIUS

Prayer of Abandonment to God

Father, I abandon myself into your hands; do with me what you will. Whatever you may do, I thank you: I am ready for all, I accept all. Let only your will be done in me, and in all your creatures—I wish no more than this, O Lord. Into your hands I commend my spirit; I offer it to you with all the love of my heart, for I love you, Lord, and so need to give myself, to surrender myself into your hands without reserve. And with boundless confidence, for you are my Father. Amen.

BLESSED CHARLES DE FOUCAULD

PRAYERS FOR COMFORT

*So let us confidently approach the throne of grace
to receive mercy and to find grace for timely help.*

HEBREWS 4:16

Psalm 121

A song of ascents.
I raise my eyes toward the mountains.
From whence shall come my help?
My help comes from the LORD,
the maker of heaven and earth.
He will not allow your foot to slip;
or your guardian to sleep.
Behold, the guardian of Israel
never slumbers nor sleeps.
The LORD is your guardian;
the LORD is your shade
at your right hand.

By day the sun will not strike you,
nor the moon by night.
The LORD will guard you from all evil;
he will guard your soul.
The LORD will guard your coming and going
both now and forever.

The Beatitudes

Blessed are the poor in spirit,
> for theirs is the kingdom of heaven.

Blessed are they who mourn,
> for they will be comforted.

Blessed are the meek,
> for they will inherit the land.

Blessed are they who hunger and thirst for righteousness,
> for they will be satisfied.

Blessed are the merciful,
> for they will be shown mercy.

Blessed are the clean of heart,
> for they will see God.

Blessed are the peacemakers,
> for they will be called children of God.

Blessed are they who are persecuted for the sake of
righteousness,
> for theirs is the kingdom of heaven.

Blessed are you when they insult you and persecute you and
utter every kind of evil against you [falsely] because of me.
Rejoice and be glad, for your reward will be great in heaven.
Thus they persecuted the prophets who were before you.

MATTHEW 5:3–12

Psalm 46:2–12

God is our refuge and our strength,
an ever-present help in distress.
Thus we do not fear, though earth be shaken
and mountains quake to the depths of the sea,
Though its waters rage and foam
and mountains totter at its surging.

Streams of the river gladden the city of God,
the holy dwelling of the Most High.
God is in its midst; it shall not be shaken;
God will help it at break of day.
Though nations rage and kingdoms totter,
he utters his voice and the earth melts.

The LORD of hosts is with us;
our stronghold is the God of Jacob.
Come and see the works of the LORD,
who has done fearsome deeds on earth;
Who stops wars to the ends of the earth,
breaks the bow, splinters the spear,
and burns the shields with fire;

"Be still and know that I am God!
I am exalted among the nations,
exalted on the earth."
The LORD of hosts is with us;
our stronghold is the God of Jacob.

Offering It Up Prayer

Dear Lord, I offer you (concern/problem/intention) for the conversion of sinners, in reparation for sins and for the holy souls in purgatory. Amen.

Prayer When Using Holy Water

(When making the Sign of the Cross.)
By this holy water and by Your Precious Blood, wash away all my sins, O Lord, *and for the holy souls in Purgatory.* Amen.

> *Do not fear: I am with you;*
> *do not be anxious: I am your God.*
> *I will strengthen you, I will help you,*
> *I will uphold you with my victorious right hand.*
>
> ISAIAH 41:10

Psalm 23

The LORD is my shepherd;
there is nothing I lack.
In green pastures he makes me lie down;
to still waters he leads me;
he restores my soul.
He guides me along right paths
for the sake of his name.
Even though I walk through the valley of the shadow of death,
I will fear no evil, for you are with me;
your rod and staff comfort me.
You set a table before me
in front of my enemies;
You anoint my head with oil;
my cup overflows.

Indeed, goodness and mercy will pursue me
all the days of my life;
I will dwell in the house of the LORD
for endless days.

PRAYERS FOR THE SICK, SUFFERING, AND DYING

Heal me, LORD, that I may be healed;
save me, that I may be saved,
for you are my praise.
JEREMIAH 17:14

Prayer for the Sick

Dear Jesus, Divine Physician and Healer of the sick, we turn to you in this time of illness. O dearest comforter of the troubled, alleviate our worry and sorrow with your gentle love, and grant us the grace and strength to accept this burden.

Dear God, we place our worries in your hands. We place our sick under your care and humbly ask that you restore your servant to health again. Above all, grant us the grace to acknowledge your holy will and know that whatsoever you do, you do for the love of us. Amen.

Father of goodness and love, hear our prayers for the sick members of our community and for all who are in need. Amid mental and physical suffering may they find consolation in your healing presence. Show your mercy as you close wounds, cure illness, make broken bodies whole and free downcast spirits. May these people close to your heart find lasting health and deliverance, and so join us in thanking you for all your gifts. We ask this through the Lord Jesus who healed those who believed. Amen.

Prayer for the Suffering

O Jesus, You suffered and died for us; You understand suffering. Teach me to understand my suffering as You do, to bear it in union with You, to offer it with You, to atone for my sins and to bring Your grace to souls in need. Calm my fears; increase my trust. May I gladly accept Your holy will and become more like You in trial. If it be Your will, restore me to health so that I may work for Your honor and glory and for the salvation of all mankind. Amen.

Mary, help of the sick, pray for me.

Prayer for the Dying

O St. Joseph, foster father of Jesus Christ and true spouse of the Virgin Mary, pray for us and for the suffering and for those who will die this day or night. Amen.

PIOUS UNION OF ST. JOSEPH

Prayer for the Dying

Most Merciful Jesus, lover of souls, I pray You, by the agony of Your Most Sacred Heart, and by the sorrows of Your Immaculate Mother, to wash in Your Most Precious Blood, the sinners of the world who are now in their agony, and who will die today. Heart of Jesus, once in agony, have mercy on the dying. Amen.

My Lord God, even now resignedly and willingly, I accept at Thy hand, with all its anxieties, pains, and sufferings, whatever kind of death it shall please Thee to be mine. Amen.

Prayer to St. Joseph for a Happy Death

~ St. Joseph is the patron for the dying.

O Blessed St. Joseph, who didst yield thy last breath in the fond embrace of Jesus and Mary, when the seal of death shall close my career in life, come, holy Father, with Jesus and Mary, to aid me, and obtain for me this only solace which I ask for in that hour, to die encircled by their holy arms. Into your sacred hands, living and dying, Jesus Mary, Joseph, I commend my soul. Amen.

Jesus, Mary and St. Joseph, I give you my heart and soul.
Jesus, Mary and St. Joseph, assist me in my last agony.
Jesus, Mary and St. Joseph, may I breathe out my soul in peace with you.

De Profundis—Psalm 130

Out of the depths I call to you, LORD;
Lord, hear my cry!
May your ears be attentive
to my cry for mercy.
If you, LORD, keep account of sins,
Lord, who can stand?
But with you is forgiveness
and so you are revered.
I wait for the LORD,
my souls waits
and I hope for his word.
My soul looks for the Lord
more than sentinels for daybreak.
More than sentinels for daybreak,
let Israel hope in the LORD.

For with the LORD is mercy,
with him is plenteous redemption,
And he will redeem Israel
from all its sins.

Glory be to the Father, the Son, and the Holy Spirit;
as it was in the beginning, is now, and ever shall be,
world without end.
Amen.

PRAYERS FOR THE
HOLY SOULS IN PURGATORY

To pray for the dead...it was a holy and pious thought.
Thus he made atonement for the dead that they might be
absolved from their sin.

2 MACCABEES 12:44–46

Prayer to the Heart of Jesus for the Holy Souls

O Gentlest Heart of Jesus, ever present in the Blessed Sacrament, ever consumed with burning love for the poor captive souls in Purgatory, have mercy on the soul of Your departed servant. Be not severe in Your judgment, but let some drops of Your Precious Blood fall upon him (or her), and send, O merciful Savior, Your angels to conduct him (or her) to a place of refreshment, light and peace. Amen.

Prayer to Mary, Queen of Heaven and Earth

O Mary, may the souls who suffer cruel torments in Purgatory, purified by the ardor of the flames, be the object of your compassion!

O Mary, Open Spring that cleanses our faults, Reconciler of sinners, reach out to those who pray to you and implore your assistance in Purgatory!

O Mary, intercede for the deceased. They await patiently the end of their suffering when they will see you and taste eternal joys!

O Mary, Model of the Just, Guide of the faithful, Salvation of those who hope in you to lead them to God, help us to pray ardently for the souls of the deceased and touch the Heart of your Divine Son!

O Mary, by the merits you have gained, give the dead true life, obtain mercy for them, and be the way which leads to your Son Jesus and to Eternal Rest! Amen.

Prayer for the Holy Souls in Purgatory

Eternal Father, I offer Thee the most precious Blood of Thy Divine Son, Jesus, in union with all the Masses said throughout the world today, for all the Holy Souls in Purgatory, for sinners everywhere, for sinners in the Universal Church, for those in my own home and within my family. Amen.

ST. GERTRUDE THE GREAT

Offering of the Holy Wounds and the Precious Blood

Eternal Father, I offer You the Holy Wounds of Your Son, and His Precious Blood,for the conversion of sinners and for the relief of the souls in Purgatory. Amen.

Prayer for All the Faithful Departed

O God, Creator and Redeemer of all the faithful, grant to the souls of Your servants departed the remission of all their sins; that through our fervent prayers they may obtain the pardon which they have always desired. Who live and reign with God the Father in the unity of the Holy Spirit, God, world without end. Amen.

Eternal rest grant unto them, O Lord.
And let perpetual light shine upon them
May they rest in peace. Amen.

Prayer for Deceased Parents

O God, who has commanded us to honor our father and our mother; in thy mercy have pity on the souls of my father and mother, and forgive them their trespasses and make me to see them again in the joy of everlasting brightness. Through Christ our Lord. Amen.

Prayer for the Forgotten Dead

O merciful God, take pity on those souls who have no particular friends and intercessors to recommend them to Thee, who, either through the negligence of those who are alive, or through length of time, are forgotten by their friends and by all. Spare them, O Lord, and remember Thine own mercy, when others forget to appeal to it. Let not the souls which Thou hast created be parted from thee, their Creator. Amen.

****

May the souls
of all the faithful departed,
through the Mercy of God, rest in Peace.

****

NIGHT PRAYERS

In peace I will lie down and fall asleep,
For you alone, LORD, make me secure.

Night Prayer

O Christ, you are the light and day which drives away the night, the ever shining Sun of God and pledge of future light. As now the ev'ning shadows fall please grant us, Lord, we pray, a quiet night to rest in you until the break of day. Remember us, poor mortal men, we humbly ask, O Lord, and may your presence in our souls e now our great reward.

<small>LITTLE OFFICE OF THE BLESSED VIRGIN MARY</small>

Short Prayer at Night

O my God, I thank you for having preserved me today and for having given me so many blessings and graces. I renew my dedication to you and ask pardon for all my sins.

> *~ Review the day, be thankful for the good things*
> *that have happened and have true sorrow for your sins.*

Act of Contrition

O my God, I am heartily sorry for having offended Thee, and I detest all my sins because I dread the loss of Heaven and the pains of Hell, but most of all because I have offended Thee, Who art all good and deserving of all my love. I firmly resolve with the help of Thy grace to confess my sins, to do penance, and to amend my life. Amen.

Psalm 51:3–21

Have mercy on me, God, in accord with your merciful love;
In your abundant compassion blot out my transgressions.
Thoroughly wash away my guilt;
and from my sin cleanse me.

For I know my transgressions;
my sin is always before me.

Against you, you alone have I sinned;
I have done what is evil in your eyes
So that you are just in your word,
and without reproach in your judgment.

Behold, I was born in guilt,
in sin my mother conceived me.

Behold, you desire true sincerity;
and secretly you teach me wisdom.

Cleanse me with hyssop, that I may be pure;
wash me, and I will be whiter than snow.

You will let me hear gladness and joy;
the bones you have crushed will rejoice.

Turn away your face from my sins;
blot out all my iniquities.

A clean heart create for me, God;
renew within me a steadfast spirit.

Do not drive me from before your face,
nor take from me your holy spirit.

Restore to me the gladness of your salvation;
uphold me with a willing spirit.

I will teach the wicked your ways,
that sinners may return to you.

Rescue me from violent bloodshed, God, my saving God,
and my tongue will sing joyfully of your justice.

Lord, you will open my lips;
and my mouth will proclaim your praise.

For you do not desire sacrifice or I would give it;
a burnt offering you would not accept.

My sacrifice, O God, is a contrite spirit;
A contrite, humbled heart, O God, you will not scorn.

Treat Zion kindly according to your good will;
build up the walls of Jerusalem.

Then you will desire the sacrifices of the just,
burnt offering and whole offerings;
then they will offer up young bulls on your altar.

Prayer for Daily Neglects

Eternal Father, I offer You the Sacred Heart of Jesus, with all its love, all its sufferings and all its merits.

First – To expiate all the sins I have committed this day and during all my life.

Glory be to the Father, the Son, and the Holy Spirit;
as it was in the beginning, is now, and ever shall be,
world without end. Amen.

Second – To purify the good I have done poorly this day and during all my life.

Glory be to the Father, etc.

Third – To supply for the good I ought to have done, and that I have neglected this day and all my life.

Glory be to the Father, etc.

****

O Jesus, Son of the Living God,
and Son of Mary,
have mercy on me, a poor sinner.

****

Watch, O Lord—Evening Prayer

Watch, O Lord, with those who wake, or watch, or weep tonight, and give Your angels and saints charge over those who sleep.

Tend Your sick ones, O Lord Christ.
Rest Your weary ones,
bless Your dying ones,
soothe Your suffering ones,
pity Your afflicted ones,
shield Your joyous ones,

and all for Your love's sake. Amen.

ST. AUGUSTINE

Prayer to Redeem Lost Time

O my God! Source of all mercy! I acknowledge Your sovereign power. While recalling the wasted years that are past, I believe that You, Lord, can in an instant turn this loss to gain. Miserable as I am, yet I firmly believe that You can do all things. Please restore to me the time lost, giving me Your grace, both now and in the future, that I may appear before You in "wedding garments." Amen.

ST. TERESA OF ÁVILA

Night Prayer

Jesus Christ, my God, I adore you and I thank you for the many favors you have bestowed on me this day. I offer you my sleep and all the moments of this night, and I pray you to preserve me from sin. Therefore, I place myself in your most sacred side, and under the mantle of our blessed Lady, my Mother. May the holy angels assist me and keep me in peace, and may your blessing be upon me. Amen.

ST. ALPHONSUS LIGUORI

****

When you awake in the night, transport yourself quickly in spirit before the Tabernacle, saying: "Behold, my God, I come to adore You, to praise You, to thank You, and love You, and to keep You company with all the Angels."

ST. JOHN VIANNEY

****

Psalm 91—A Prayer of Divine Protection

You who dwell in the shelter of the Most High,
who abide in the shade of the Almighty,

Say to the LORD, "My refuge and fortress,
my God in whom I trust."

He will rescue you from the fowler's snare,
from the destroying plague,

He will shelter you with his pinions,
and under his wings you may take refuge;
his faithfulness is a protecting shield.

You shall not fear the terror of the night
nor the arrow that flies by day,

Nor the pestilence that roams in darkness,
nor the plague that ravages at noon.

Though a thousand fall at your side,
ten thousand at your right hand,
near you it shall not come.

You need simply watch;
the punishment of the wicked you will see.

Because you have the LORD for your refuge
and have made the Most High your stronghold.

No evil shall befall you,
no affliction come near your tent.

For he commands his angels with regard to you,
to guard you wherever you go.

With their hands they shall support you,
lest you strike your foot against a stone.

You can tread upon the asp and the viper,
trample the lion and the dragon.

Because he clings to me I will deliver him;
because he knows my name I will set him on high.

He will call upon me and I will answer;
I will be with him in distress;
I will deliver him and give him honor.

With length of days I will satisfy him,
and fill him with my saving power.

The LORD bless you and keep you!
The LORD let his face shine upon you, and be gracious to you!
The LORD look upon you kindly and give you peace!
Numbers 6:24–26

NOTES ON *BELOVED*

The Holy Rosary

"Rosary" comes from the Latin word *rosarium*, meaning "garland of roses" or "crown of roses." We offer a spiritual "bouquet of roses" to the Blessed Mother every time we pray the rosary. Mary lovingly intercedes for each of us as she presents our intentions before the throne of God to her Son, Jesus. Our prayers are always answered. Perhaps not as we expected (or desired) them to be, but "no prayer ever went unheard, and our Blessed Lady has never been known to fail."[1]

The rosary is a simple and beautiful prayer that brings reconciliation, peace and inner joy. It was a favorite prayer of Blessed Pope John Paul II. "From my youthful years this prayer has held an important place in my spiritual life. The rosary has accompanied me in moments of joy and in moments of difficulty. To it I have entrusted any number of concerns: in it I have always found comfort."[2]

Blessed Pope John Paul II wrote in his apostolic letter *Rosarium Virginis Mariae:* "To recite the rosary is nothing other than to contemplate with Mary the face of Christ."[3]

The rosary helps us to be conformed ever more closely to Christ until we attain true holiness."[4] When you pray the rosary with all your heart you will experience an "outpouring of love."

The Stations of the Cross

"Moreover, the great saints all affirm that meditation of the passion and death of Our Savior is the most fruitful that one can engage in."[5]

The Way of the Cross

To journey through life, in imitation of the one who "endured the cross, despising its shame, and has taken his seat at the right hand of the throne of God" (Hebrews 12:2).[6]

> ~ *Excerpt from Blessed Pope John Paul II's*
> *opening meditation and prayers*

BIBLIOGRAPHY TO NOTES

1. Lacey, Charles V. 1954. *Rosary Novenas to Our Lady.* (Mission Hills, California: Benziger), 6.
2. Blessed Pope John Paul II. *"Rosarium Virginis Mariae*, Apostolic Letter on the Most Holy Rosary, No. 2." Available online at vatican.va.
3. *Ibid.* No. 3.
4. *Ibid.* No. 26.
5. The Stations of the Cross, Explanation and History. Diocese of Palm Beach. Available online at: diocesepb.org/the-stations-of-the-cross.
6. Pope John Paul II. "Stations of the Cross at the Colosseum. Good Friday, April 21, 2000, Opening Prayer." Available online at vatican.va.

CPSIA information can be obtained at www.ICGtesting.com
Printed in the USA
LVOW05s2059160214

373849LV00003B/8/P